Explorations in Language Study
General Editors:
Peter Doughty   Geoffrey Thornton

LANGUAGE IN BILINGUAL COMMUNITIES

Derrick Sharp

EDWARD ARNOLD

© Derrick Sharp 1973

First published 1973
by Edward Arnold (Publishers) Ltd.
25 Hill Street, London W1X 8LL

ISBN: 0 7131 1789 3

Already published in this series

Language Study, the Teacher and the Learner
P. S. Doughty and G. M. Thornton

Explorations in the Functions of Language
M. A. K. Halliday

English as a Second and Foreign Language
B. Harrison

Language, Brain and Interactive Processes
R. S. Gurney

Language in the Junior School
E. Ashworth

Printed in Great Britain by Butler & Tanner Ltd,
Frome and London

General Introduction

In the course of our efforts to develop a linguistic focus for work in English language, now published as *Language in Use*, we came to realise the extent of the growing interest in what we would call a linguistic approach to language. Lecturers in Colleges and Departments of Education see the relevance of such an approach in the education of teachers. Many teachers in schools and in colleges of Further Education see themselves that 'Educational failure is primarily *linguistic* failure', and have turned to Linguistic Science for some kind of exploration and practical guidance. Many of those now exploring the problems of relationships, community or society, from a sociological or psychological point of view wish to make use of a linguistic approach to the language in so far as it is relevant to these problems.

We were conscious of the wide divergence between the aims of the linguist, primarily interested in language as a system for organising 'meanings', and the needs of those who now wanted to gain access to the insights that resulted from that interest. In particular, we were aware of the wide gap that separated the literature of academic Linguistics from the majority of those who wished to find out what Linguistic Science might have to say about language and the use of language.

Out of this experience emerged our own view of that much used term, 'Language Study', developed initially in the chapters of *Exploring Language*, and now given expression in this series. Language Study is not a subject, but a process, which is why the series is to be called *Explorations in Language Study*. Each exploration is focused upon a meeting point between the insights of Linguistic Science, often in conjunction with other social sciences, and the linguistic questions raised by the study of a particular aspect of individual behaviour or human society.

Initially, the volumes in the series have a particular relevance to the role of language in teaching and learning. The editors intend that they should make a basic contribution to the literature of Language Study, doing justice equally to the findings of the academic disciplines involved and the practical needs of those who now want to take a linguistic view of their own particular problems of language and the use of language.

Peter Doughty
Geoffrey Thornton

Contents

Introduction

A major theme of this series is that Language Study, properly considered, is a many-sided activity. In order to answer the question, 'How *do* men use language to live?', it must embrace a wide variety of different approaches to language and its use. Thus the series includes some titles which discuss the concept of Language Study itself and its educational implications; others which make a direct contribution to our understanding of the nature and function of language; others which focus upon a major field of language teaching or language learning; and others which offer a detailed study in depth of one aspect of using language to live. The present volume is our first example of this last approach, a study of bilingualism in one community, Wales, a study of how people in one community make use of two quite distinct languages in the normal course of their day-to-day activities.

As Derrick Sharp suggests, the interest lies partly in the fact that the bilingual speaker does not draw upon the whole range of resources each language offers him; and partly in the fact that his use of either language, at any one time, is determined by the total situation of speaking, both who is present and what is talked about. The bilingual speaker, let us say, enters into the same range of activities as any other human being, but, when he comes to make use of language, he will draw upon one language for some of these activities and another for the remainder. Whereas the speaker who has only one language will find himself using a wide range of different varieties of that language, according to his situation of speaking, the bilingual speaker will find himself moving, not just from one variety to another, but from one language to another.

The more important issue from the teacher's point of view, however, and the main focus of the book, is what happens to language for learning in the schools of a bilingual community. What is to be the language of instruction? What relationship is established between the two languages, in the context of the classroom and in the school as a whole? As Derrick Sharp points out, one crucial factor is the relationship between the two languages in the local community of which the school is a part. Another, and perhaps ultimately more important, factor, however, is the relative status of the two languages, judged in relation to the world community of languages.

The particular interest of a study of the situation in Wales is that the two languages concerned are so very different in their relative status. Welsh is the valued cultural possession of a relatively small number of speakers, concentrated geographically, whereas English is a World Language. In this, Welsh is representative of a large and growing number of bilingual situations, where speakers of a mother tongue of comparatively restricted distribution find themselves having to function in a social and cultural context dominated by a World Language.

As Derrick Sharp makes clear, that is a sense in which 'each bilingual community is unique', but his work shows how much we have to gain from this close focus on one community if we want to understand the general nature of the problems which arise in all such communities. There are important social and cultural parallels, moreover, between the bilingual community, properly so called, and the increasingly familiar situation in this country where local communities contain populations who speak English as a foreign language. The parallel may be drawn even more closely where children are born and grow up in this country speaking Urdu or Hindi or Hausa as the language of the home and English as the language of the community at large.

As we are now a member of the European community, it may not be fanciful to suggest that the day is not far distant when our schools will include many who speak, as their native tongue, the languages of continental Europe, thus making bilingualism a phenomenon likely to enter the experience of very many teachers.

Finally, the classroom in the bilingual community may have much to show us when we focus upon the question of language for learning in our complex contemporary society, a society made up of a multiplicity of communities, each with its own recognizable pattern of social and cultural habits, its own ways of viewing the world, and consequently its own ways of using language to live. Where the bilingual pupil finds himself using one language at

8

home and another at school, very many pupils in our society have to use in school a variety of their one language which is so very different from the variety they use at home, that the psychological, cultural and educational effects upon them may be very similar to those which the bilingual pupil experiences. It is never true to say, as many public figures and some teachers do, that these pupils 'speak a different language'; it is, however, worth any teacher's time to consider what he can learn about the effect of this wide divergence between pupils' language for living and the language they are asked to use for learning by looking at the bilingual situation, where all the relevant features are so sharply accentuated by the division of activities between two distinct languages.

Peter Doughty

1 The nature of the task

This book has been written for teachers and students in training in order to clarify some of the issues involved in language teaching and learning in bilingual communities, to identify the problems, and to suggest what are considered to be profitable lines of thought and future inquiry. It relates the newer ways of looking at language and languages developed by modern linguists to work in the classroom and practice in the school, particularly in a bilingual situation, and suggests which research findings and academic ideas are of immediate relevance and assistance and which can be seen as remote from the classroom in present circumstances, usually because results so far are inconclusive.

An example of this is the effect on a bilingual of his bilingualism, about which there is still very little firm evidence, although we are coming to appreciate more and more the importance of attitudes and their impact on the educational system, and living in a bilingual community rouses strong feelings about language in most people. Our main concern must be with the educational and social effects of bilingualism, and the relationship between the two. How are a bilingual's thinking processes affected by his command of two languages at a similar level of proficiency? Are the effects different according to his standard of general ability? What significance attaches to the age at which he learns his second language? What is involved in switching languages in a bilingual community where all are not bilingual? Does this differ in kind from code switching as practised in all languages? The answers to these and related questions will determine our language policy in schools and our language teaching methods.

Each bilingual community is unique, just as every situation in which language is used is unique. This is not to deny certain similarities amongst communities, whether we are looking at large countries, small closely-knit societies or immigrant populations in large cities in the United States of America or England. Nor does it ignore common factors which occur in all language learning and teaching contexts, whether we are concerned with a first, second or foreign language, either singly or in combination. Any teacher faced with language teaching and learning problems in whatever situation can have light thrown on his difficulties by an examination of those encountered by others in entirely different contexts. There is certainly no suggestion that the study of one bilingual community has no bearing on practice in the others, but the only practicable and acceptable procedure is to move from the particular to the general as far as one can. The range of linguistic backgrounds found in the classrooms of Wales, for instance, will be paralleled in other bilingual situations, but the patterns will be different and for the teacher the problems will vary according to the nature of the two languages, both intrinsically and dependent on their relative status, and the solutions will depend on such factors as the degree of formality traditional in the teaching methods of the particular community.

Wales is therefore taken as an example for detailed examination, because most of the problems of bilingualism and bilingual education can be studied in this country. Chapter 2 establishes a foundation by looking at certain aspects of the language situation relevant to later detailed study of the problems, while each of the following chapters takes one area of concern to educationalists. No attempt has been made to avoid some overlapping of these areas, for it is considered helpful to look at the same problems from different points of view. Although many of the points made are relevant to both languages, that is, the total situation, English is chosen for close examination because it is the first language for the majority and an essential second language for the minority who need to be bilingual, and because it figures as one of the two languages in many bilingual communities, not only the large ones like South Africa but also the very small ones like the Gaelic-speaking community in the Outer Hebrides. Recently developed approaches to the teaching and learning of English should be of interest to all these communities.

The relationship between language and society is always a most complex one, for even in a unilingual society each individual in the course of a day adjusts his language usage many times to suit the company he is in, the task in hand, the nature of the communication and his purpose or purposes. It would be inappropriate here

12

to explore all the complexities, but the point is that in order to lead a full and satisfying life he has to master not one language but many varieties, or codes, of it. As he develops, he makes progressively fewer mistakes in his code-switching, and he becomes more proficient at 'placing' people socially and professionally by their language usage, just as others are 'placing' him and adopting the appropriate code. Most of us gain the ability to switch codes by experience, sometimes bitter, and the process continues throughout life. Comparatively few of us never become very proficient at it. This constant interaction in any society means that language is inextricably involved in all societies with social and cultural patterns which in most cases have been formed over many years and which are constantly changing. When we are concerned with two languages of comparable or different status in a bilingual community the problems which arise are inevitably more complicated and extensive.

The reasons for many features of bilingual communities and the strong feelings generated are to be found in history, and will vary from country to country, as will the language policies adopted. The social, political and religious aspects are therefore of vital importance, whether we are considering Wales, Belgium, Canada or South Africa, but this book cannot hope in a small compass to deal with them as such. They are borne in mind, however, as far as they impinge on the schools, mainly in areas of policy, for no consideration of education can be divorced from the society in which the system operates, just as language in the same context must not be considered in the abstract or in isolation from the wider sphere in which it is used.

There is also no discussion of whether there should be bilingual education for those who are native speakers of a minority language. It is assumed that such a language and the culture of which it is part merit preservation, even though the task becomes increasingly difficult in the face of developments in communication and the consequent increasing domination by the world languages, and of advances in technology which are economically possible only if they cater for large masses of people. All the factors tilt the scales heavily in favour of the world language when it is side by side with a minority language in a bilingual situation, and minority groups therefore need special treatment in education as in other spheres such as radio and television. The extent to which they receive such special treatment is ultimately a political decision, of course, but even within the educational system much may be done by the way in which available resources are allocated. In Wales, for example, Welsh first-language textbooks are not commercially viable in the same way as English texts are in England, because the potential audience is comparatively so small, making it very difficult, even with the guaranteed sale system, to provide the full range and choice which are desirable. Welsh second-language and English second-language textbooks encounter similar difficulties.

Because motivation and attitudes are so important in a bilingual community, the demands made by those who are genuinely and deeply concerned about the preservation and extension of a minority language become a matter of nice judgment. If they seek special treatment too enthusiastically, they may cause a reaction against the minority language and stand even to lose ground. We shall see in Chapter 2 that pupils' attitudes towards the two languages change as they grow older, English gaining favour and Welsh losing it on average. In these circumstances is it good policy to demand that all schools in Wales should be fully bilingual, or that Welsh should be compulsorily taught to all pupils throughout their school careers, remembering that the majority of the population have English as their first language? The answer depends on many factors, including the quality of methods and materials for teaching Welsh as a second language, but surely any realistic policy must allow for varying conditions from area to area and school to school? Global demands are less likely to succeed than steady and continued persuasion within the realms of immediate feasibility, but the question above gives a measure of the complexity of some of the problems to be encountered within, as well as outside, the educational system. There must be long-term aims, but there are no simple solutions to the more controversial problems inherent in bilingual communities.

Indeed, solutions to any of the problems are hindered by our limited knowledge. Thus the handicapping effects of bilingualism on general school progress, detected in some researches, may be the result not of bilingualism itself but of accompanying social conditions which could be ameliorated in some cases and to some extent. Much more investigation is needed, but we cannot wait on the facts. We are now more capable of identifying the problems, and we must work to solve them in the light of present knowledge, modifying and adapting as the picture becomes clearer. It may well be that bilingualism has a beneficial effect on the individual's school progress when other factors in the environment are held constant or compensated for in an assessment. Improving social conditions is a matter partly of government action, and it could be a generation or two before changes have any noticeable effect. More rapid progress can be made, while this larger process is in hand, at local authority or school level, because some factors are under the direct control of those working in the educational system. An individual teacher, or one school, can take the initiative pending decisions and action on a larger scale.

As has been made clear, solutions will vary according to local conditions and the basic philosophy of the particular educational system. In Wales the imposition of one detailed scheme is out of the question, partly because of the diversity of the linguistic areas and therefore of the schools, and partly because the teacher by tradition retains a large measure of professional freedom and choice. Nevertheless, common aims and agreed policies, arrived at in principle by discussion, have an important place to occupy if there is to be overall progress without conflict or confusion. Elsewhere, one unified scheme covering the whole situation might well be the best solution, especially where the bilingual community is very small and is part of a system with a larger measure of central control than exists in Britain.

Before looking in detail at the various aspects, it might be helpful to draw up a list of those problems which we can attempt to solve within the educational system, covering matters of policy concerning the two languages in the schools of a bilingual community. The list is not intended to be exhaustive, nor will all items on it be covered in the following chapters, but it does include the most important issues and gives a synoptic view of language problems in bilingual communities.

1. Language policy

   Should the aim be full bilingualism for all members of the community?
   Should the study of both languages be compulsory at all stages?
   Should the policy vary according to the linguistic background of the individual, or of the area?
   What special consideration do the native speakers of a minority language need?

2. The language medium of teaching

   Should all pupils be taught sometimes through the medium of their second language?

If so, at what age should second-language medium teaching be introduced, and on what system?
Should there be a full choice of medium in higher education?

3. Language teaching methods and materials

What are the special requirements of a situation covering both first and second language approaches to two languages?
How do the nature and status of the two languages affect decisions?
What light is thrown on these matters by the findings of modern linguistics?
What is the role of language study?

4. The use of the two languages in the general life of the school

Should the school have a consistent policy on this?
Should all activities and functions be bilingual whenever possible, or should one language be used for some, the other for the rest?

5. Parental involvement

Should parents have the choice of sending their children to a bilingual or to a monoglot school?

6. The language education of teachers

What special provision should be made for the training of all teachers in bilingual communities?
What is needed by those who teach one or both languages?
How do the problems of initial training differ from those of in-service training?

7. Supporting services

Should bilingual schools, especially small ones, have a more favourable pupil/teacher ratio?
What is the special function in bilingual communities of language advisers or local inspectors?
What should be the relationship between teachers and research workers?
What contribution can teachers' centres make?

These representative questions reflect the language problems found in all bilingual communities, and the rest of this book will be devoted to an extended discussion of most of them. No specific

16

mention is made of multilingualism, but by extension the problems may be seen as similar in kind though even more complicated in nature.

For the teacher in a bilingual community these are urgent, pressing problems, but an examination of them in one context has a much wider validity, not only for those in other bilingual situations but also for all who are concerned with language learning and teaching anywhere. We shall not find solutions if we become obsessed by the difficulties, great as they may sometimes be, nor shall we succeed if we continually wait upon further knowledge, much as we need it. Above all we must have a true appreciation of the nature and function of language in society so that we may clarify our thinking about all those situations in which pupils are using contrasted ways of speaking.

2 The language situation in Wales

Although each bilingual community is unique, this detailed examination of certain aspects of language learning and teaching in Wales will reveal features which also occur in other bilingual situations, such as those in Canada and Belgium, for example, and may suggest lines of approach capable of wider application. It is equally true that experience in other bilingual communities, as well as in the fields of English as a second language and as a foreign language, especially in work with immigrants in England, is of value to those concerned with language work in Wales. In all areas the obvious need is for more knowledge about language and about children, more research and curriculum development work designed to relate the latest findings of linguistics, psychology and sociology to the language learning situation, both inside and outside the school. Nowhere is this need greater than in the case of the learning of English by children whose first language is Welsh, for, although much good work is done in the field of English as a second language in Wales, it is not firmly based on linguistic studies, it is not carefully planned over a period of years, and it depends on the special interest and enthusiasm of a teacher, or group of teachers in an area, or of a language organizer. The factors which have caused, and still cause, this comparative neglect of English in the educational system of Wales will emerge later in the chapter.

The first step in any assessment of the language situation in Wales is to attempt to determine the linguistic nature of the various areas according to the proportions of Welsh speakers, but this apparently straightforward process is very difficult to carry out with any degree of accuracy. One aspect of the sampling procedure of the Schools Council Research and Development Project on 'Attitudes to and motivation for the learning of Welsh and English in

Wales' (in the rest of this book referred to as the Attitudes Project) illustrates the difficulties and also indicates the range of linguistic areas to be found. A stratified random sample of schools throughout Wales was used for the administration of attitude scales and questionnaires in the autumn of 1969, and the first classification of schools was based on the linguistic background of the areas in which they were situated. The latest figures available when the sample was drawn up were those given in *Census 1961: Report on Welsh Speaking Population*, and it was appreciated that these would serve only as a guide, because of the lapse of time and the imprecise nature of the questions asked in the census. Nevertheless they did, and do, give as good a picture of the distribution of Welsh speakers as can be achieved at present. The proportions of Welsh speakers were charted on a map of Wales parish by parish, and each Local Education Authority (LEA) was classified according to the proportion of Welsh speakers within its geographical area. Pockets of significant linguistic difference within LEA areas were considered separately, as were Rhondda Borough and the eight Divisional Executive Districts of Glamorgan. The specially created bilingual schools ('Welsh schools') were placed in a separate category, as the linguistic background of the areas in which they are situated is not reflected in the schools; they are mentioned here because they are an exception to the general school pattern discussed later.

LINGUISTIC BAND A

Carmarthenshire
Merioneth
Anglesey
Cardiganshire   } 68–81% Welsh speakers.
Ystradgynlais
North Pembrokeshire
Caernarvonshire

LINGUISTIC BAND B

West Glamorgan Division
Denbighshire (except Wrexham)   } 48–55% Welsh speakers.
Montgomeryshire (except
   Newtown and Welshpool)

Breconshire (except Ystradgynlais)
Neath and District Division
Aberdare and Mountain Ash Division
Rhondda
Port Talbot and Glyncorrwg Division
Merthyr
Flintshire
Mid-Glamorgan Division
Swansea
Caerphilly and Gelligaer Division
Pontypridd and Llantrisant Division
South Pembrokeshire
South East Glamorgan Division
Cardiff
Wrexham
Newtown
Welshpool

} 3–26% Welsh speakers.

This distribution gives some measure of the linguistic variations from area to area in Wales, and shows why it is possible to refer to predominantly Welsh-speaking areas (Band A) and anglicized or predominantly English-speaking areas (Band C). It also indicates the size of the educational problem if the recommendation of the Gittins Report that a fully bilingual policy should be pursued is to be implemented. One other immediately relevant point is to be found in that Report:

. . . it must be remembered that English is the second language of some 16 per cent of children in Wales.

This estimate, made in 1967, leads us from a consideration of the total language picture to an examination of the school situation. The figures given above show a range throughout Wales from 3 to 81 per cent Welsh speakers, and the linguistic background of the area in which the school is placed naturally affects its policy, but the crucial factor is the proportion of Welsh first-language (W1) pupils. At one extreme, schools in highly anglicized areas will have no or very few W1 pupils, while, at the other, all the pupils in a small primary school in a predominantly Welsh-speaking area will be W1. In between these extremes all the possible mixtures exist, the problems being probably most acute for those schools with a small but noticeable proportion of E1 pupils in an otherwise W1 population, or vice-versa. The teaching medium is determined by the predominant native language of the pupils, a straightforward process where the groups are homogeneous or divide naturally into first-language groups of approximately class size, but the difficulties arise when the minority group is not large enough to be treated as a separate unit. The possible complications are obvious. In addition, other factors operate in some circumstances, LEA policy and the pupil's age and choice of subject being obvious examples. The existence of a bilingual school in the area also affects the situation, for such schools tend to attract those teachers and pupils with a great interest in and concern for the Welsh language, so that both W1 and W2 work is often more limited in the other schools as a consequence.

In this complex situation it can fairly be said that the teaching and learning of English have not received enough consideration; for Welsh, the language of the minority, though historically the national language, has had to press its claims forcefully in order to survive and, hopefully, to develop. It is understandable that most attention in recent years has been given to the teaching of Welsh as both first and second language, and that in some quarters there has been an emotional reaction against and comparative neglect of English, which it is argued is strong enough to take care of itself. This attitude, however, is less than fair to W1 pupils, who deserve the best methods and materials which can be devised for all their studies. English in the schools of Wales embraces both first and second language approaches, though except in the early stages and for purposes of discussion these cannot be completely separated, for they merge increasingly as the child's proficiency in English develops. First-language problems are equally present in second-language work in the later junior school stages and in the secondary school, because W2 pupils have considerable and increasing contact outside the school with native language uses of English, particularly on radio and television. At the other end of the scale, we are concerned with E1 pupils whose environment is entirely English, as far as the language is concerned. And this is the situation before we consider the effect of two cultures.

Cultural considerations complicate still further the language pattern already outlined, though as always there is no clear polarity involved. It would be possible, though not profitable, to distinguish in Wales further divisions than the main ones into Welsh, Anglo-Welsh and English traditions and ways of life, so that to speak of two cultures is to over-simplify. Although the niceties of argument do not all concern us here, one comparatively minor problem which results is the question of the choice of literature to be studied in schools. More importantly, a crucial question with direct educational implications is whether the Welsh language is an integral and therefore essential part of Welsh culture, for on the answer to this depends the language policy to be adopted in the schools. The Gittins Report (11. 3 'Language, culture and community') considers the main arguments clearly and concisely, reaching the conclusion that:

Although a Welshman is what he is without the language, since he takes part in the ways of life and traditions of Wales, and vicariously lives in the language, he would, we feel, be a fuller Welshman if he possessed his ancestral tongue.

As a consequence, the Report advocates a bilingual policy in the schools of Wales, and is relevant here because of its bearing on the status of and provision for English. Without further examination of the cultural aspects, though bearing them in mind, let us consider the language policies which operate in the various areas of Wales.

Because the language policy in its own area is the responsibility of each LEA, it is impossible to be precise and up to date at any given moment, as the picture is constantly changing. Authorities naturally review their policies from time to time, and tend to do so more particularly after the publication of a major report such as that mentioned above. Most changes are minor and rarely occur simultaneously in a large number of areas, however, so that the pattern discovered in the autumn of 1969 by the Attitudes Project may be taken as a fair reflection in general terms of the present position. (Monmouthshire and Radnorshire did not take part.) At that time only one LEA stated that it did not have a language policy, but it was in the process of defining its policy and discussing its practice of leaving the teaching of Welsh in primary and county secondary schools to the discretion of headteachers, while making Welsh compulsory for all pupils in the first two years of grammar and comprehensive schools. Although all the other LEAs had language policies, these varied greatly in nature and effectiveness of implementation; in several cases the statement of policy was vague, without clear definition of aims or provision for the teaching of Welsh, while one authority mentioned the difficulty of ensuring that each of its primary schools had a member of staff able to implement its policy of providing Welsh lessons for all pupils at that stage. Other statements were precise. For example, one LEA serving mainly anglicized areas said that Welsh was taught to all except backward pupils, that bilingual schools or classes were established where there was demand, and that all teachers involved in the teaching of Welsh had to have a thorough knowledge of language teaching methods and techniques. Another which included large anglicized towns stated that the language better known to the child on admission should be the main medium of instruction for that child, but that the minor language should be introduced orally at the age of five and used increasingly as a medium of instruction for some other subjects. As was to be expected, most authorities in predominantly Welsh-speaking areas had thorough-going Welsh language policies, whereby Welsh was taught throughout the schools, and used extensively as the medium of instruction for both W1 and W2 primary school pupils. The aims of these authorities were worthy of note, for two of them intended to ensure 'reasonable facility' in both languages by the time of transfer to secondary education, and a third desired that all pupils should be completely bilingual, and not merely proficient in their second language, by statutory school-leaving age. In two areas both Welsh and English were taught to school-leaving age or to GCE 'O' level. The general concern throughout Wales was illustrated by the fact that only three LEAs had no official responsible for implementing language policy. Two authorities had full-time language organizers, while the others gave the task to someone, most often the primary schools adviser, who devoted part of his time to it. Similarly, four LEAs required their primary school teachers to be able to speak Welsh fluently, two others demanded it of 50 per cent of such teachers and a further two for those appointed to predominantly Welsh areas.

If we turn from the broader picture of authority policy to a more detailed scrutiny of practice in the schools, we are again struck by the many variations, indeed by the vast range of school policies. Headteachers of the schools in the Attitudes Project sample were asked to complete a questionnaire seeking information about many aspects of the teaching and use of Welsh and English in their schools. Completed forms were received from 52 secondary schools and 145 primary schools, spread throughout Wales. Two aspects, the teaching of Welsh and the use of Welsh as a medium of instruction, may be taken as indicative of the possibilities. Welsh was taught as a subject in all but three (2·1 per cent) of the primary schools, though it must be remembered that the amount of time devoted and the importance attached to the subject would vary considerably from area to area and school to

23

school. In the anglicized areas there was almost no primary school use of Welsh as a medium, while in the predominantly Welsh and the 'mixed' areas only 13 schools out of 98 used Welsh as a medium for more than 75 per cent of the time and even in these areas 37 schools used Welsh as a medium for less than 25 per cent of the time, including 16 which did not use it at all. It should be remembered that many primary schools in Welsh and 'mixed' areas are small or very small.

The secondary schools are in general larger and more complicated in organization, of course, so that the patterns revealed in 1969 were more interesting and helpful. The effectiveness of a language policy depends just as much on what happens in the later stages, and it could be suggested that so far too much of the attention has been given to the initial and early stages. The fact that many authorities give responsibility for language policy implementation to the primary schools adviser may be significant. Only one of the 52 schools sampled did not teach Welsh as a subject, though 8 of the heads failed to complete this part of the questionnaire. Classes were organized in one of two ways, either separately for W1 and W2 pupils, or in mixed groups. Schools in Welsh areas tended to adopt the first method, whereas mixed language groupings were usual in the anglicized areas, where the percentage of fluent Welsh speakers was very small. The specially created bilingual schools were an exception, for they taught Welsh and English equally to mixed first and second language classes, though later three of the four vetted their pupils according to ability in Welsh. Two of these schools also had a crash course for first-year pupils whose command of Welsh was insufficient for general school purposes, including Welsh medium teaching.

It is difficult to generalize about the use of Welsh as a medium of instruction at the secondary stage, for it was naturally found only in the Welsh areas, and by no means in all schools there. Indeed, in some of these areas Welsh medium instruction was deliberately limited to one school and pupils allocated accordingly. In most schools using Welsh certain classes were taught through this medium while parallel classes were taught in English. Most schools also had different policies for different subjects, using Welsh for part or the whole of each course in each year and for a varying number of years. In a number of schools the whole of the religious education course was taught through the medium of Welsh at all stages. Other subjects most frequently indicated as being taught in Welsh were history, geography, physical educa-

24

tion, craft and music, whereas those least frequently indicated were mathematics, science and English. The most systematic approach to Welsh medium teaching was found in the four bilingual secondary schools, as might be expected. All four taught religious and physical education in Welsh at all levels, and history and geography for five years; three taught craft, music and domestic science completely in Welsh. One taught all the subjects mentioned so far and classical and modern languages completely in Welsh, and mathematics, science and English completely through the medium of English. Two others taught mathematics, science, English, classical and modern languages partly in English and all other subjects entirely in Welsh, while the fourth school used less Welsh to teach the older age-groups.

The variations in policy and practice discerned in this brief examination of the language situation in Welsh education reflect the British system of local government and the traditional freedom of the teacher to determine his own content and method. Inevitably the question arises as to whether a more unified approach would be more effective. Any attempt to impose common policies and methods would of course be doomed to failure and in any case unrealistic, because of the considerable differences in linguistic background from area to area of Wales. But there is surely everything to be gained from greater co-operation and frequent discussion amongst those concerned at all levels in the system, so that decisions may be taken in the light of knowledge and pooled experience. The number of occasions on which teachers and educationalists meet to discuss areas of common concern has increased rapidly in recent years, but, even in the sphere of language policy, the Welsh aspects of which have received a great deal of attention, much remains to be done. The process of arriving at agreed aims and schemes, with the essential element of choice built in, is a slow one, but it is the only practicable way of improving language education in a bilingual community such as that under consideration.

For solutions to the language problems of Wales are not to be reached by logical analysis alone. The gloomiest forecasts suggest that Welsh will have disappeared as a living language by the end of this century, and many who are less pessimistic are nevertheless deeply concerned about the struggle for continued and extended existence of a minority language in competition with a major world language which is the native language of the majority of the population. It is natural, therefore, that feelings should run high and that stands should be taken on both sides, based largely or exclusively on emotional rather than logical arguments. Because the importance of attitudes in this situation was appreciated, the main aims of the Attitudes Project were to establish pupils' patterns of attitude towards Welsh and towards English, and to examine the relationship between attitude and attainment. Attitude tests were administered to a stratified random sample (approximately $6\frac{1}{2}$ per cent) of three age-groups, the fourth year in the junior school and the second and fourth years in the secondary school, and then attainment tests in Welsh and in English were given to a sub-sample of each age-group. It is not appropriate here to go into the detail of research techniques, but some of the findings proved relevant to the general theme of this chapter. Attitude patterns of the kind anticipated were clearly established, and it was found that the mean scores of attitude towards each language were modified with age; as the pupils grow older attitude towards Welsh tends to become less favourable and attitude towards English more favourable. Thus the learning situation for English improves with age, certainly as far as motivation is concerned. A most interesting discovery was that pupils throughout the sample were viewing English in two distinct ways. If they made an objective assessment of it the results were uniformly favourable, whereas if they considered it in the context of Wales their attitude towards English sometimes became unfavourable as a result of a favourable attitude towards Welsh. Thus in the schools the key attitude is that towards Welsh, for fluctuations in attitude towards English are a direct reflection of attitude towards Welsh. The pupil's linguistic background proved to be the most highly significant source of variation in attitude, and of those variables examined it is the only one capable of being modified in the school by policy decisions. Of equal relevance to the teaching situation in schools is the finding that attitude towards the first language, whether Welsh or English, was significant in relation to attainment at the age of 10+, was much less significant at 12+ and was not significant at 14+, whereas in direct contrast attitude towards Welsh as a second language was highly significant in all groups, although less so at 14+ than in the two younger groups. In first language attainment the most significant factor was general ability, as assessed by teachers.

The implications of the factors identified in this brief outline of the language situation in Wales will be dealt with in later chapters. The intention has been to illustrate by example the complications which exist and which influence decisions about language education in a bilingual community, though the reader may consider that other aspects, such as parental attitudes and the administrative costs of alternative schemes, are of greater importance. It is impossible to measure, and even perhaps identify, all the factors involved. Amongst teachers, particularly some of those in predominantly Welsh areas and of those elsewhere who are vitally concerned about the Welsh language, the situation may in extreme cases lead to a refusal to accept the need for work or in-service training on the teaching of English. The writer was told on one occasion by a small group of teachers that they knew how to teach English and thought that the time and effort ought to have been devoted to Welsh, in order to reduce the inequalities in status between the two languages. Extreme opinions of such a nature are comparatively rare, but there are others who see English as a threat to Welsh because they consider that true bilingualism is impossible for the majority and that Welsh will occupy the subordinate position as a result of the practical arguments in favour of English. At the other end of the scale are those who maintain that the Welsh language is for all practical purposes dead already and who think it should be buried as soon as possible; in between comes every shade of attitude conceivable. The total effect of these opinions cannot be gauged, but they exist and must be taken into account in any discussion of language teaching and learning in Wales.

The real debate, then, is between those who favour an educational policy of bilingualism, with its obvious extension into the life of the principality, and those who would prefer to see English as the sole official language in the schools and life of Wales. Although there are strong arguments in favour of a full bilingual policy in the schools (see the Gittins Report), the position of English will not be affected for the next generation or two of pupils whichever policy is adopted. It is beyond dispute that every pupil in Wales, whatever his linguistic background, needs to develop proficiency in English to the best of his ability, but this is not to suggest for one moment that development in English should be at the expense of Welsh in any way whatever. Not enough is yet known about the best ways of developing proficiency, and this is particularly true of English as a second language in Wales, but the way ahead lies in the improvement of methods and materials rather than in, for example, the devotion of more school time to the subject. One would expect the basic principles of first language work to remain the same in varying situations, so that the differences between Cardiff and Merioneth would compare in kind with those between Birmingham and Cornwall, but again not enough is known about the detail and the effect of the presence of another culture based on another language. Welsh as a second language has been receiving increasing attention, quite rightly, and the inevitable development of sophistication amongst teachers in their language work is to be welcomed. Similarly, any improvement in English methods and materials, both second and first language, will be of general as well as specific benefit. Some of the possible approaches will be considered in the following chapters.

3 The particular problems of bilinguals

In concentrating on the language problems in the schools of Wales it is as well to remind ourselves from time to time of the wider issues in the bilingual community, those issues which may be called cultural, political and religious and which, though difficult to examine in any precise way, operate crucially in particular forms from time to time and at all times influence educational policy. The purpose of this chapter, however, is to move in the other direction and look not at the school system, LEA policy or teaching methods but at the individuals most closely concerned, the pupils in the schools. What are the particular language problems faced by bilingual pupils as individuals or groups? Are they the same for E1 as for W1 pupils? What is the effect, if any, on a monoglot living and working in a bilingual community? These are key questions, and it must be stated at the beginning that the answers to them are not at all clear in the present state of knowledge, although progress has been made in defining relevant areas for study and in suggesting fruitful lines of development.

If we accept as a basis for discussion the figures given in the Gittins Report, we can say that 84 per cent of the pupils in the schools of Wales have English as their first language. We do not know how many of these also have a command of Welsh, although most of them will have been taught Welsh at some stage in their school careers, perhaps not very well or very enthusiastically in some cases. But it is reasonable to suggest that the number of W2 speakers with at least some fluency is at the moment rising, partly because of the rapid development in W2 teaching methods and materials in recent years, partly as a result of work such as that being carried out by the Schools Council Research and Development Project in Bilingual Education, partly as a consequence of the less specifically educational efforts of various groups in the principality.

Amongst this majority group of E1 pupils there will clearly be varying degrees of bilingualism, quite apart from those who for various reasons have no Welsh at all. Of those with Welsh, some will use it fluently and frequently in daily contacts, some will use it occasionally in particular situations, some will use it very rarely, perhaps as a 'party piece', and some will never use it at all once they have left the classroom; but for all of them Welsh is, and almost without exception will remain, a second language. Very few of them will develop equal proficiency in both languages, and probably none will switch from E1 to W1.

For the 16 per cent of pupils for whom Welsh is the mother-tongue the situation is both simpler and more complicated. It is simpler because all of them will learn English as a second language and will achieve a degree of fluency in it by the time they move into the secondary school stage, so that in this sense they will all be bilingual. It is more complicated because English does not remain for all a simple second language in the sense that Welsh does for E1 pupils. For some it will do so, but for many it will become of equal status and use with Welsh, and for some again it will supplant Welsh as the mother-tongue. The practical need to learn English is the cause of this difference, and one important factor is the increasing exposure to English outside the school, notably on television, though by no means exclusively, as was illustrated by one girl in north Wales who said, 'We need to learn English in order to be able to speak to tourists.'

This analysis is of interest in three ways. It reinforces the account given earlier of the vast range of linguistic backgrounds found amongst pupils in the schools and emphasizes the need for a corresponding range of language learning and teaching techniques. By illustrating the complex situation in another way it indicates a possible danger in that teachers may become too concerned about the differences between the two languages and amongst pupils, perhaps at the expense of recognizing the central role of the native language in child development; a bilingual community needs greater awareness of the principles and practice of mother-tongue teaching because of the possibilities of confusion mentioned later. And it focuses attention on the definition of the word 'bilingual', which is used with so many different meanings.

At this point it would be as well to pause and consider this difficult matter of definition, for enough background information has been given for the classroom aspects to be appreciated. Remember that Wales is typical of those bilingual communities in which one world language and one local minority language are found, and that although there are others with two languages of comparable status, as in Switzerland and Canada, most of the educational problems of bilingualism can be studied in the Welsh situation. The term 'bilingual community' in fact presents no problem, for it is clearly used to describe a country or area in which two languages are used by substantial proportions of the population, with varying numbers of people needing or desiring to use both. Thus bilingual communities include Wales, Ireland, Belgium, Switzerland, Canada and South Africa. But there is another type of bilingual community, usually of more recent development as far as it concerns the classroom today, brought about by the comparatively large mass immigration of groups from other lands with other mother-tongues. Such groups are found in parts of the United States of America and in England, particularly London and the Midlands, for example. The similarities between the two types are marked, mainly because similar processes have taken place in different periods of history, but there are also features which distinguish the two, such as the more urgent need of the immigrant to learn the language of his new home. In the classroom, therefore, immigrant children may be highly motivated and yet easily discouraged by lack of immediate success, while the social factors which operate in all learning situations seem often to bear heavily on such children. The nature of bilingual communities is a fascinating topic for discussion; it must be sufficient at this point to state that each bilingual community is unique and has its own language problems, but that these problems may be of the same kind as those encountered in other communities, and for this reason the study of problems and practice in one area has a wider application.

In contrast to the ease with which we can grasp and accept the concept of a bilingual community is our difficulty in defining the bilingual individual, indicated earlier in this chapter by the use of the expression 'varying degrees of bilingualism'. The range found in the classroom, described above, is the kind of pattern to be expected in all bilingual situations, though it should be noted that for practical, educational purposes there are no monoglot Welsh speakers, those few who do exist being very old or very young. The majority of the population may be classified as monoglot English, with a command of Welsh, if any, restricted to greetings and perhaps a hymn or national song, but amongst the minority will be found those equally fluent in both languages and those for whom

English is and remains a second language. Precise figures are not available, but there is an understandable tendency where one language is world-wide for that language to dominate the minority language, however deeply rooted the latter may be. Thus in Wales, for example, there are cases of language shift from W1 to E1 but the reverse movement is very unlikely to happen; similarly children in Welsh-speaking communities use Welsh much more frequently when talking to adults than they do amongst themselves, in contrast to language habits only a generation or so ago. In these situations, therefore, the preservation of the minority language becomes a matter of decision, particularly within the educational system, and is always a controversial issue, as in Wales. As a result a great deal of time and energy is often devoted to an attempt to define a bilingual, the desired end-product of a particular type of education, and while the distinctions made by scholars, such as that between compound and co-ordinate bilinguals, are of interest and a proper contribution to knowledge they do not provide an easily-applied solution to the problem faced by all students of language in bilingual situations. If one wishes to conduct a survey to determine, let us say, the number of W1 children in the schools of a given area, or the number of fourteen-year-olds who are fully bilingual, how does one decide the criteria to be adopted? Two methods are commonly used: the judgment of an experienced expert, perhaps the headteacher of a junior school, and the administration of linguistic background and language attainment tests. In a large-scale survey the second method achieves a desirable consistency, in contrast to the differences of judgment amongst a group of experts, but both methods are open to objection by those who reject the findings of the survey because they do not accept the basic system of classification.

By now it should have become clear that much of the debate about the true nature of a bilingual is remote from the classroom, even though some schools may need or wish to organize their classes on a first-language basis, or an Authority may wish to determine the success of its bilingual policy. These two examples are deliberately different in kind, and the second will be taken up again later. In practice the first type of decision is made in the light of experience, either individual or pooled, perhaps in consultation with the pupils and/or parents, perhaps in some cases with outside help, such as the use of a published Linguistic Background Scale. In practice this works well enough, with no more difficulty than that experienced by the teacher who is asked to name the bilingual children in his class. Naturally the more help that can be provided by research the better, just as the more a teacher knows about language and the problems of bilingualism the better, but doubt about the precise definition of a bilingual is not an obstacle to further discussion.

All teachers know and accept that although one aim of education is literacy not all pupils will attain the same level in this area, and some will fail to achieve even basic proficiency. Amongst those who become literate, a wide range of mother-tongue ability will be observed at the end of schooling and later in adulthood. In the same way bilingual education must expect varying degrees of bilingualism amongst its pupils, for in addition to the many individual, social and educational factors operating in the case of literacy there are those factors peculiar to the bilingual situation. It may be argued that all pupils except the educationally subnormal are capable of becoming literate, but it is at least open to argument that there are some pupils above ESN level who will never achieve bilingualism in an acceptable sense and who will be handicapped in their general school progress by any attempt to make them bilingual. The problem is then one of identification, of course, and must be taken into account in the formulation of a bilingual policy.

'An Authority may wish to determine the success of its bilingual policy.' This leads on to a consideration of the bilingual from a slightly different point of view. What should be the standards by which we judge the progress of a bilingual in each of his two languages, and how do these standards compare with those of mother-tongue learning at the different stages? It seems logical to suggest that the individual's progress in his first language should correspond to that of mother-tongue pupils elsewhere, but it is not realistic to expect the E1 child in a predominantly Welsh area to reach the same standards in the junior school as his counterpart in England, for example, and the teacher needs to take this into account. On the other hand, the E1 child in an anglicized area should be expected to achieve normal mother-tongue standards, for although he may, and probably will, learn some Welsh in school he does not *need* to become bilingual, so that whether he does so or not is a matter of choice. The position is very different, however, for the W1 pupil, because he, like all minority-language pupils in similar bilingual communities, *must* learn the world language for very many practical reasons. More than this, he needs by the time he leaves school to achieve a standard of fluency

assessment

comparable with that of native speakers of English, and so we have a realistic aim for bilingual education. But the ways in which he learns English will be different, particularly in the early stages, and we must not expect him to catch up in reading and writing, or indeed in fluency, vocabulary and idiom, by the end of the junior school. It is widely assumed that the vast majority of W1 pupils do become in effect native speakers of English by the time they move to the secondary school, and certainly the best do, but there still remains a need for an E2 approach for many pupils in secondary schools in predominantly Welsh-speaking areas. Nor must the schools be satisfied with what might be called academic proficiency in English, whereby the bilingual has an excellent command of written English but a more limited grasp of spoken English, especially in its less formal styles. This has often occurred in the past, but is less likely to happen now and in future because of the increasing emphasis on oral work in all language learning and teaching, and the consequent compensation in school for the bilingual's limited *use* of English in his community, as opposed to the amount he reads or hears on radio and television.

The implications for teaching will be dealt with later, but at this point we can say that the educational system must attempt to ensure that all native speakers of the minority language are fully bilingual by the end of their school careers. It may be desirable for other reasons that all members of the community should be fully bilingual, though that is a separate and usually political issue. We then come back to where we started, and must ask ourselves what standards are realistic and how we measure a bilingual's language proficiency. At present there is no satisfactory complete answer, though the many language surveys carried out in Wales do suggest partial solutions and profitable lines of approach. This is not the place to deal with these surveys in detail, though a study of them indicates the size of the total problem, and in most cases their validity has been questioned on grounds suggested earlier. One example may be taken to throw light on this discussion, however: the objective survey carried out in 1958 by the Merioneth Education Committee in order to determine whether the standard of English attained by the age of eleven was satisfactory. There were several relevant features, one of which was the realistic standards adopted: it was considered satisfactory if by the age of 10 + the E1 group had reached a standard within three months of the standard of attainment to be expected of an English child in England—and the W1 group had reached a standard within

34

twelve months of that attained by the E1 pupils as a group. Apart from a Language Questionnaire and standardized tests, the survey included a subjective assessment of oral proficiency, which revealed striking differences in this respect from school to school. The results as a whole did show that the attainment was satisfactory according to the criteria adopted, and that there were interesting differences between urban and rural areas and between the Welsh and English groups. The conclusion to be drawn from these differences is that in L2 learning an adequate supporting linguistic background makes a great contribution to success; e.g. the widespread use of English in the environment, particularly in towns, was a vital factor. A further survey of the same children was carried out three years later. This showed that by the age of 13 + the level of attainment in English in the county was very nearly equal to that expected of English children in England, a highly satisfactory state of affairs.

A note of caution was sounded in the two reports, however, and it must be repeated here. There was no objective test of a vital area of language ability, the capacity of the children to express themselves freely and fluently in the second language in both speech and writing. Complete objectivity in oral and free writing tests is very difficult to approach and impossible to achieve in the present state of knowledge, but it is in these very aspects that experience and observation suggest that L2 learners are likely to be least competent, as opposed to their mastery in the secondary school of the 'academic' aspects mentioned earlier. The implications for the syllabus are clear. The Attitudes Project also found that for Wales as a whole there were no significant differences in English attainment between the W1 and E1 pupils in the 12 + and 14 + samples, but here again this result was based solely on objective tests, for no oral test was included and the pupils wrote a free composition only in their first language. It should be remembered that in all surveys of this kind the results show what might be called a picture of the average. For the teacher the encouraging side of the picture is that many pupils will achieve much higher standards, but this is balanced by the fact that an equal number will fall short of 'satisfactory' and need greater attention and better methods than they have perhaps received in the past.

One further example of the way in which surveys have been both helpful and incomplete in the consideration of standards and comparative attainment will suffice. The table given on p. 273 of the Gittins Report shows greater differences than those mentioned so far, but it is concerned solely with English reading ability:

National Survey of Reading, England and Wales, 1957, comparison of scores in English reading of differing linguistic groups.

Table 12.5.2

	Score points English reading	
	11 years	15 years
All Wales	12·0	20·8
First language Welsh pupils	9·4	18·0
Others	12·4	21·4
All England	13·3	21·7
Urban	13·6	22·1
Rural	12·1	19·2

(A difference of one point is approximately six months of reading age.)

In fairness, the comments made in the Report should also be quoted:

These are averages based on a sample of children tested in 1957, with some degree of variation or error. It must be borne in mind that the Welsh-speaking bilingual children had normally had two years less English. In addition, many of them would be found in rural areas, which have a higher proportion of families at the lower social-occupational levels. . . . The rural-urban difference is seen clearly in the results for England too.

These results suggest that, at about 11, bilingual Welsh speakers are approximately 18 months behind monoglot English children in Wales in English reading and 23 months behind English norms. In view of the fact that they have mastered two languages and not begun reading in English until about 7, bilingual Welsh-speaking children have made good progress. Nevertheless, the difference in score between the various language groups remains at age 15. Moreover, if it is true that over a third of children in England have still not wholly mastered reading by 7, this does raise fundamental questions about the difficulties which may be encountered by Welsh-speaking children, who, in addition, begin to learn reading in the second language.

36

This extract provides a measure of the achievement of those children in a bilingual modern society such as Wales who have to master a world language in addition to their native tongue, while at the same time it indicates the difficulties faced by bilingual children and their teachers. Furthermore, it raises questions, the first of which will be dealt with in a later chapter. Should W1 children start reading (and writing) English at such an early age as 7? The second question is germane to the theme of this section. To what extent is reading ability indicative of general language ability in English? It might be that the differences shown above would be greatly exceeded if we could test the powers of fluency and free expression described already, and although a body of expert opinion believes that this would be so, equally it might not. Such questions, and the related one of what kind of understanding and control of each language we want bilingual children to have, emphasize the need for more knowledge in this complicated and crucial area.

Faced with this task of attempting to achieve native language proficiency in two languages, the bilingual child runs the risk of confusing the two, and in extreme cases suffering comparative failure in both, so that he may be said to have two second languages. Educationalists are well aware of the interference effects between pairs of languages in this situation and a great deal of attention has been paid to them. Without doubt they do operate, so that the patterns of one language are imposed on the other by both children and adults. Sometimes the interaction produces a new and distinct language, as in the West Indies and New Zealand, but more usually the effects are limited, as they are in Wales, where the results are the Welsh dialect of the English language and the adoption and absorption by many Welsh-speakers of English words and phrases. Much depends on the nature of the two languages. Because Welsh spelling is phonetic we should expect young W1 children to experience difficulties with English spelling, and this was in fact the aspect of English in which the Merioneth children referred to above were least proficient, but we must remember also that English spelling is notorious for causing trouble to all learners, including the English. An awareness of interference effects is valuable to teachers planning language programmes so that they may give due attention to the difficulties. One function of research is to provide this kind of information, which for school purposes is best obtained by error analysis rather than by comparative linguistic analysis, in order to ascertain which aspects of interference actually do present problems to the learner. But it can be argued that our educational thinking has attached too much importance to interference, which is generally concerned with the details of language. It would be going too far to suggest that the confusion experienced by bilinguals is no greater than that of the monoglot learning two foreign languages, but intensive practice in the second language, of the kind now accepted as vital in first and foreign language learning, will produce better and more rapid results than language exercises concentrating on areas of interference. Certainly in Wales it would seem that in practice confusion is a transitional, early stage through which the vast majority pass safely and without undue trouble. Although we must concern ourselves with the minority who do not, we can to some extent at least treat them separately, bearing in mind that methods found successful with them may also speed up the progress of the majority.

Another feature of bilinguals is what may be called language zoning, their tendency to use one language habitually in certain contexts and the other in equally clearly defined situations. The concept is familiar in all language usage as code-switching, the ability to adapt one's language to varying demands and changing situations, but it is particularly heavy in its pressure on the bilingual to master a wide range of language usage in both his languages. Many monoglot pupils remain limited in their mother-tongue range of codes, and most learners of a foreign language are extremely limited in range; this emphasizes the task facing the bilingual and his teacher. Obviously when he is speaking to a monoglot the bilingual's language is determined for him, and this can be a handicap if he lives and works in a majority language area, but otherwise his language usage may be divided in various ways: he may use his first language at home and in local social activities, and his second language at work and in social activities connected with his job; in his home environment he may always use one language when talking to people of an older generation, and the other with contemporaries and younger people; he may use one language only in chapel; and so on, the possible variations being many. The usage is often not logical, as in the known case, typical in principle, of the woman who used Welsh to the milkman and the cat, and English to everyone else, including her husband and daughter, who were also Welsh-speaking.

Such zoning in language usage is natural for a bilingual, as is code-switching in all use of language, but in some few cases amongst

38

adults it can indicate a limitation which is found as a transitional stage in the early days of a young child's progress from being a monoglot to being fully bilingual. The limitation operates if the bilingual is *unable* to use the alternative language in a particular context, revealing a restriction which is another indication of the difficulty in defining bilingual. Range of usage in the second language is as important as quality of usage, and for obvious reasons many bilinguals are limited in their L_2 usage. Others in situations such as that in Wales move from one area to another and find that their opportunities for L_1 usage are few, so that their L_2 usage improves in range and quality, perhaps to the extent that the individual's languages change places, L_1 becoming L_2, and vice-versa.

The importance of usage in a wide range of contexts suggests the action that the school should take in bilingual education. Language must be based on experience in a two-way process, so the school must provide intensive spontaneous practice in the second language during the vital early years in the infants and junior school. To begin with, and for some considerable time, the spoken language must occupy a central position, the teacher providing in the classroom opportunities for interaction in the second language appropriate to the stage of development of the pupils, perhaps to compensate for the lack of such interaction outside school. In Wales, as in similar bilingual communities, there is an increasing amount of English in the W_1 child's total environment. This does not necessarily mean that his opportunities for using the language increase steadily, though often this does occur, but it does mean that there is a strong supporting background for his E_2 learning. Contrast the situation of the W_2 learner in an English language area in Wales, who will have few if any opportunities to use or even hear Welsh outside school. The prevalence of English in the Welsh language areas, except the remotest, has implications for E_2 teaching methods. W_1 pupils, except those who are competent bilinguals on entry to school, need E_2 methods in the early stages, but on average they will become native speakers of English by the age of 13 and at some stage between the ages of 5 and 13 E_2 methods will become inappropriate and E_1 methods appropriate. This transition does not occur at the same point in all cases, obviously, though for ease of class teaching it has been usual to take the average and in general terms switch to E_1 methods at the age of transfer to secondary education (11 +). What is needed is a carefully graded language programme which starts as E_2 and

39

gradually introduces E1 while equally gradually phasing out E2, recognizing throughout the child's other native language. Such a programme would be suitable for class teaching with reasonably homogeneous classes, but it could also have the advantage for the teacher that it would allow individual or group progress according to ability, maintaining E2 methods into the secondary school for the slower children. It is difficult to be precise, and out of place here, anyway, but these points will be taken up again in the chapter on language teaching methods.

In our attempts to explore bilingualism we must next ask ourselves how being bilingual affects the individual, and particularly whether any effects are advantageous or disadvantageous. There has been a great deal of research into the relationship between bilingualism and intelligence and attainment, but the results are often contradictory, mainly because of two problems encountered by those conducting surveys. The first has been dealt with already: the difficulty of defining bilingualism and a bilingual. If investigators are using different criteria for the classification of language types, we must expect the results to vary, hence the need for all concerned to make clear the basis of their categories. The second problem is common to all research in education and the social sciences: how can we isolate bilingualism as a variable from all the other factors in the total situation? Can we be sure that an observed effect is caused by the fact of being bilingual and not, for example, by home background, father's occupation or school policy and teaching methods? At present we cannot be sure, although research techniques are steadily improving and the statistical method known as analysis of variance provides us with firmer answers than were possible even a generation ago.

In Wales there have been many systematic investigations since the work of D. J. Saer, an Aberystwyth headmaster, which was first published in 1922, but the testing language itself, now seeming so obvious as likely to affect results, was not appreciated as a factor until the work of Ethel M. Barke in 1933. She was the first to use non-verbal intelligence tests because she realized that bilingual children are most likely to suffer by comparison with monoglots in the area of language, especially if verbal intelligence tests in the second language (in this case English) are used. There were also deficiencies in the interpretation of results in early investigations, as sophisticated statistical techniques were not, and could not at that time be, applied. Subsequent work in Wales, notably that of W. R. Jones, has increased our knowledge of the problems and

40

indicated some solutions, though the number of factors involved and differences in time and geography amongst the various investigations raise doubts about the extent to which general conclusions may be drawn. If this is true for research in one bilingual community, the reader can readily appreciate the extreme caution necessary when any attempt is made to relate findings in different communities.

Nevertheless, it is possible to suggest that the research evidence indicates that bilinguals do not suffer by comparison with unilinguals in non-verbal tests of intelligence. Research into comparative attainment in the two languages and in other school subjects, though equally contradictory and inconclusive, does lead us to believe that some of the measured differences are at least partially caused by decisions on policy and teaching methods, and not by bilingualism itself. Thus if we fail to provide the W1 pupil with plenty of practice in free expression in English, and then give him an English free composition test, we should not be surprised if his performance disappoints us and falls short of his achievement in Welsh free composition. Similarly, the bilingual apparently runs considerable risk of mental confusion, but this may not be an inevitable consequence of his situation; it is more probable that it is caused by the introduction of reading and writing in his second language before these skills are firmly established in his first, and/or the use of the second language as the medium of instruction too early in his school career. It is significant that those children who have achieved an appropriate mastery of the two languages before entry to school suffer few of the disadvantages experienced by those who first encounter the second language as a school subject. It is at least a working hypothesis, too, that the effects of bilingualism depend on the individual's level of ability, so that, as in all spheres of learning, any adverse effects will be felt most severely by the pupil of low ability, who needs more attention than he has traditionally received. Few workers would claim that the bilingual child has an advantage in I.Q. tests or any other sphere, though there was a slight suggestion in the Attitudes Project results for one age-group (12 +) that a bilingual background in some way helped or promoted the learning of English.

The research evidence is generally inconclusive, therefore, but one point with practical implications emerges from it. The educational system cannot change some of the variables involved in the bilingual's total situation; it cannot alter sex or home background, for example, but it can change those variables within its control, notably school language policy and teaching methods, and it is clear that these are influential in the bilingual's development. Second language methods and materials are crucial, while basic research must continue in order to determine the effects of changes made. School language policy is equally important, and the Attitudes Project findings suggest a line of approach which might well prove helpful.

In certain circumstances the deliberate fostering of the minority language, even at the apparent expense of the other, will lead to a healthy development in both languages. It would seem that the world language is in a sense able to take care of itself, though this in no way contradicts the point made before that second language methods must be developed as fully as possible. In all areas of Wales there is a strong English language supporting background, but in many areas the equivalent Welsh language background is weak or even non-existent. If the school is committed to a bilingual policy, from either necessity or desire, it can attempt to compensate for the weak outside background by an increased use of the minority language in its own affairs, both general activities and teaching medium, bearing in mind all the time that attitude to Welsh is vital in determining attitude to English, as described in the previous chapter. This means that one would not introduce an extensive use of Welsh as a medium in a school where the pupils' attitude to Welsh was in general highly unfavourable, because there would naturally be an even greater reaction against the language and one's purpose would be defeated at once. On the other hand, there is much to be said for increasing the use of Welsh in a school in which the pupils have a generally favourable attitude to the language, at least as an experiment in bilingual education.

The suggestion, made before by others for different and often controversial reasons, is prompted by the survey results of one type of school, the specially created bilingual ('Welsh') schools, established in the anglicized areas to cater for those desiring a fully bilingual education. At the crucial secondary stage these schools have thorough-going though not uniform Welsh language policies, described in Chapter 2. They were the only schools in any of the categories to show an average attitude to English which was unfavourable. In spite of this, their English attainment was very good, while their achievement in Welsh was excellent, the W2 pupils approaching very close to W1 standards by the age of 14+. The vast majority of these pupils leave school fully bilingual, and it would seem that the 'natural' bilingual schools in predominantly Welsh-speaking areas might adopt similar language policies with beneficial effects. But as always certain reservations must be made. At the time of the survey, only five bilingual secondary schools were in existence, one of which was not included because it was in its first year, and it is possible if not probable that if the number were substantially increased the law of diminishing returns would operate. These schools at present enjoy certain advantages, for in very general terms they can be selective in their entry, they can attract a higher proportion of dedicated and efficient teachers, and their level of parental interest and support is higher than is usual even in Wales. Nevertheless, the success of their language policy does suggest that it would be worthwhile to try their methods in other types of school, carefully chosen at first, not only in Wales but in similar bilingual communities.

The picture presented in this chapter, one of the need for more knowledge, experiment, research and curriculum development, could be interpreted as depressing, but rather it is stimulating and challenging, for much has been and is being done throughout the bilingual world. Some aspects are peculiar to this world, particularly the need to handle two languages side by side and the special educational provisions required when a minority language is in competition with a world language in circumstances which favour materialistic arguments, but other problems are essentially the same in nature as those encountered in any classroom, whatever the language. These include the difficulties of grading language work to suit the age and ability level of the pupil, of ensuring that all pupils develop as complete and wide a mastery of language as possible, and of making all language work in the classroom real and fully related to the society in which it takes place. Schemes and methods must be based on sound linguistic and pedagogic knowledge, and this drawing together of ideas about the nature of language and classroom experience will be the theme of the following chapters.

4 Language teaching methods

Before considering the kind of language teaching called for both explicitly and implicitly in Chapter 3 it might be as well to deal with an aspect of especial concern to bilingual communities, the language to be used as the medium in the schools. Nowadays we are aware that even in a monoglot community the kind of language chosen as the medium can have a crucial effect on educational progress, and we hear a great deal about the gap of incomprehension between the teacher's middle-class language and the pupils' working-class language, about restricted and elaborated codes. Obviously to express the problem in these terms is crude, over-simplified and extreme, but it does serve to draw attention to an area of language usage of immediate, practical concern to all teachers which has been almost completely ignored in the past. The teacher in a bilingual community faces such problems which-ever language is used as the medium, incidentally emphasizing the need for a wide range of usage in both languages, but in addition there is the choice of one language or the other as the main medium of instruction. The brief description of Welsh-medium teaching given in Chapter 2 illustrates that the choice may not be a simple one, though usually at the primary stage one language is chosen as *the* medium. In contrast, the familiar pattern in the secondary schools is of variation from subject to subject and activity to activity, but we do not know for either stage to what extent both languages are used during a single lesson, though we do know that the practice is widespread and has much to commend it. The compli-cated pattern which results in Wales, with its general tendency to abandon the minority language as medium at a comparatively early stage, is typical of similar bilingual communities in which the educational system is not rigid and authoritarian, and where many decisions are left to the individual school or teacher.

There is a wide measure of agreement throughout the bilingual world that the earliest stages of schooling not only must but should be conducted through the medium of the child's mother-tongue. This works well in the majority of cases, but it can cause difficulties of two kinds. There are bilingual communities in which it is not easy to secure enough teachers proficient in the minority language and qualified in other respects, though concerted efforts in training teachers or crash courses in the relevant language for established teachers can provide a practical if not ideal solution in a relatively short time. For a minority of pupils the difficulties can be more severe. They are those who live and go to school in an area where the predominant first language is not their own.

In Wales the W1 pupil in an E1 area is more likely to be at least partially bilingual on entry, unless he has recently moved, and in any case he needs to become bilingual at some stage during his primary school career. Certainly he needs to learn English quickly for school purposes, just as the E1 pupil in a W1 school needs to learn Welsh quickly, although in another area he might not have learnt it at all, or in a desultory fashion. Even so the Welsh pupil of either linguistic background is better off than his counterpart in some other bilingual communities, for example the Maori, who may well have to leave his own closely-knit society if he wishes to pursue his education beyond the elementary stage. It is difficult to estimate the size of the problem, for we are concerned here with a minority, obviously enough, and while such pupils 'survive' in their schools it would be unrealistic to devote large resources to their particular needs. We just do not know to what extent they are handicapped in their general school progress as a result of their particular language problem, but we can suggest that the total effect may be masked because the weaker pupils will suffer most and their failure at school may be attributed to other factors, particularly general ability, especially if this is tested in the 'wrong' language.

Without doubt it is the native speakers of the minority language who fare worst in this kind of situation in a bilingual community, for whereas all the teachers in a minority language area will be fully, or at worst adequately, bilingual and can ease the worries of the pupil from the other linguistic background, the same is not universally true of the world language areas. In Wales the aim of most Authorities in anglicized areas is to have at least one Welsh-speaking teacher in each primary school, but it is not always possible to achieve this, modest as it seems. The only complete

45

solution, that of demanding that all teachers in a bilingual country should be bilingual, is impracticable, partly because at present it is usually difficult to find sufficient bilinguals to staff the schools in the bilingual areas, partly because such a policy would devote a disproportionate amount of the educational budget to meet the needs of a minority within a minority. It could be argued on political grounds, but that is beyond our scope here. At present educational authorities in all countries must concentrate on the central issues, perhaps in the hope that a proper system of bilingual education will in time provide its own solution to the problem of pupils outside their native language areas. In the meantime, minority language pupils in major language areas should receive sympathetic treatment, especially in the choice of school to which they are sent. The alternative solution, that of creating special bilingual schools in world language areas, is more practicable and has other advantages as well, as has been made clear in the previous chapter.

Pupils may experience individual or small group difficulties with the language medium, therefore, but for the vast majority the initial medium is the mother-tongue. For the native speakers of the world language it will continue to be so throughout the period of schooling, unless special circumstances or parental wishes intervene. For the native speakers of the minority language, however, the major language needs to be introduced as the medium at some stage. The purist could object to this statement, of course, maintaining that this *need* not be so, but if we take the situation in Wales as representative, we can appreciate the reasons for the prevalence of English-medium teaching. Quite apart from the historical causes, which are strong and deplored by many, a complete educational course from infants school to first degree entirely through the medium of Welsh would not be attractive to many who could take advantage of it. It is possible at the moment for a limited number to pursue such a course in some subjects, but it does severely restrict the choice of subject, university and future career, while it is significant that even the specially created bilingual schools teach certain subjects, notably mathematics and science, through the medium of English. The difficulties are many and the economic arguments in favour of English are strong, so for all practical purposes the W1 pupil needs English-medium teaching.

The crucial question then becomes at what stage it should be introduced. There are two opposing schools of thought and practice. One argues that because the pupil will meet new, technical

46

subjects, taught through the medium of English, in the secondary school, he should become accustomed to the language medium well before he leaves the junior school; English medium teaching should be introduced as early as possible. The other, concerned for the preservation of the minority language, argues that because English-medium teaching will be predominant in the secondary stage, Welsh-medium teaching should be maintained as long as possible, i.e. until the end of the junior school. Both approaches seem wrong in principle, though they may be modified in practice: the first because there is no doubt that second-language medium can be introduced *too* early and lead to confusion in the pupil's mind, just as reading and writing in the L2 can be started too soon; the second because the change-over is abrupt and at a point decided on other grounds than those of language development. The use of the language as medium is obviously dependent on the pupils' progress in learning it, but if the L2 learning has started in the infants school then L2 medium teaching can be brought in very gradually in the junior school. At first L2 may be introduced incidentally alongside L1, but there are disadvantages in this method and it is better to designate times when the L2 is to be used exclusively, building up to perhaps two whole days a week in the fourth year of the junior school. The pattern must be flexible so that it can be adapted to suit the needs of individual children and classes. The teacher, too, must be able to respond to the immediate situation, knowing when a refusal to use L1 at a time set aside for L2 is justified and when it will lead to a complete breakdown in the lesson.

As we should expect, the use of a second language as teaching medium has a marked effect on progress in that language. All that has been said applies equally whether the first language is the minority or the majority one, though it may be difficult to implement L2 medium teaching in a majority language area, where there often is indifference or even hostility to the minority language. Experiments in Wales have shown the beneficial effects on the acquisition of W2 of an alternate medium scheme, while current work indicates that indifference or hostility can more easily be overcome by involving parents and children fully from the beginning of schooling. These points link with the tentative suggestion made in the previous chapter about the use of Welsh as a medium in the secondary school in any consideration of a bilingual policy, and lead us next to second language teaching and learning.

In Wales, as in any similar bilingual community, the school has the responsibility of ensuring that its pupils can acquire the appropriate second language in an orderly, progressive way. The principles of L2 teaching and learning will remain the same whatever the situation, but methods and materials may vary considerably in detail according to local factors and the nature of the two languages. E2 in Wales may be treated too casually, getting less attention than it deserves, because a few W1 children arrive at school with a good command of English, others will acquire it rapidly because of outside influences, including the home, and all will be supported in their learning by the amount of English in the environment. Teachers of E2 may concentrate on developing better methods and materials, knowing that their W1 pupils, almost without exception, are well motivated towards learning English and that their attitude towards the language becomes more favourable on average as they grow older.

The teacher of W2 is faced by a very different situation. His E1 pupils will become on average less favourable towards Welsh as they grow older, while in most areas only a minority of parents will support him in his endeavours. He must capture the interest of his classes and not only maintain but also increase it over the years, a very tall order indeed. One dull, ineffective lesson is significant, a series of them can mean that the pupils will abandon the study of Welsh as soon as they can, and they are unlikely ever to return. Nor is his task made easier by the comparative shortage of exciting reading matter suitable for the W2 learner, especially in the crucial 12 to 14-year-old group. Despite these difficulties and the active opposition of those who regard the learning of Welsh as a second language as a waste of time, considerable progress has been made in this field in recent years, by using a simplified vocabulary (Cymraeg Byw), by developing teaching schemes, by providing graded reading materials, by courses and conferences for teachers, and above all, perhaps, by placing the emphasis on oral proficiency in the early stages and maintaining it alongside reading and writing later. By now teachers of W2 are well aware of the need to involve the children and retain their interest, and are coming more and more to realize that if W2 can be introduced in the infants school simultaneously with other educational activities they can counter their opponents' arguments about wasting time and distracting the children from 'serious' education. There are important implications here for all minority languages in comparable situations, and those who seek further detail should consult *Towards Bilingualism* and the work of the Schools Council Bilingual Project, for example.

What second language approaches are in use at present, and which are the most profitable? Mr W. R. Jones, in *Bilingualism in Welsh Education*, tabulates five possible methods which give us a convenient starting point, because each of these is in operation in one or more parts of the world, and each can be found in use in Welsh schools, either as the sole method or as one component in various combinations. It is worth noting that the somewhat confused pattern in Wales reflects both the greater freedom of British teachers and the lack of consultation and co-operation which has prevailed until very recently.

1. The traditional, formal method, including language exercises and perhaps grammar. Although largely discredited in Britain nowadays, because it is excessively intellectual and remote from the living language, it persists in both first and second language work even here, as is witnessed by the number of new textbooks which are in essence based on it and which sell well. Some teachers who have abandoned it speak of it with nostalgia, no doubt because it provides clear-cut teaching content and progressive schemes of work, however wrong or irrelevant these may be by the standards of modern linguistics and language development.

2. The direct method. Quite rightly, the extreme form in which the use of the mother-tongue was forbidden no longer survives, but properly modified it can be successful with younger children who do not have to sit external examinations which demand knowledge of grammar and the written language. Its emphasis on oral work, units of meaning, expression and appreciation of wider context of the language commend it to many, especially those who seek an everyday, conversational command as opposed to an academic, formal command.

3. The reading method. First developed in Dacca, it concentrated on reading ability, considering that speech and writing were less urgent needs for E2 learners. It was based on simplified vocabulary and graded reading materials, and was influential in America and in Wales (for W2), where it still features in principle in current thinking and practice.

4. The oral method. In its rejection of all reading and writing in the early stages, this method appears similar to the direct, but its emphasis is solely on 'systematic progression along strictly controlled lines', so that free conversation is not included. It was first

advocated by H. E. Palmer, and depends on linguistic knowledge of the particular language to provide the framework for the detailed structuring of the learning sequence. So far no complete school course has appeared because the task of acquiring the basic knowledge and the expertise to develop it into a learning system is a considerable one, but work along these lines is continuing.

5. The bilingual method. Developed by C. J. Dodson, of Aberystwyth, this method uses the development of concepts in the mother-tongue, as opposed to direct experience, as the basis for L2 learning. The teacher gives the stimulus in the mother-tongue and the learner responds in the target language, until he can dispense with the mother-tongue concept foundation and think in the L2. The author claims that this is not a translation method, but rather that 'concept-interpretation' takes place from one language to another. In spite of considerable success with the method, the theoretical basis obviously remains controversial.

Mr W. R. Jones concludes that no one method is intrinsically superior to the others, and suggests that local circumstances will determine which is most likely to succeed. This is undoubtedly true, but in the past there has often been too great an element of chance in the choice of method, insufficient preparation and perhaps understanding on the part of teachers and purely ad hoc, subjective tests of the results. We do not know enough at present about all these matters. A sixth method should be added for consideration, that developed by Miss June Derrick and her project team for use with immigrant children in England (see *Scope 1* and *Scope 2*). This does not use linguistic sequencing but rather a progression of appropriate language experiences carefully devised to lead the pupil rapidly to mastery of English for both his immediate and long-term needs. Although it would be possible to extend the list by including other developments and variations on these themes, enough has been given for our purposes.

When alternative teaching methods are laid out for inspection, however briefly and simply, it becomes clear that each has something to offer and we can understand why teachers have been attracted by this feature of one method and that feature of another, putting them together in their own syllabuses. Sometimes this approach has been highly successful, but the outcome must always remain doubtful for a very simple reason, that the features are justified in their original contexts by a theoretical foundation. This may be acceptable or not, but certainly if it is not grasped the resulting amalgam of aspects from different methods is likely to founder because of its lack of a unified base in theory. On the other hand, some features are not tied to particular methods, usually because they have a much wider application in all theories of language and language learning. One example of this is the structure found in the first method above. However misleading and ineffective it may be, the traditional, formal method does give the teacher firm ground on which to work, it enables him to see where he is going and to test his pupils' progress to date, and by its emphasis on rules it leaves him no areas of doubt or choice, provided he does not ask fundamental questions. The primacy of speech, and therefore an emphasis on an oral approach, is another aspect which is not tied to any limited context.

Which second language approach should be adopted, then? The quick, though not helpful, answer is the one which works in local conditions. Although it contains a valid point, it begs the important questions, but it also suggests that the topic cannot be considered in the abstract. For this reason we shall concentrate on the teaching and learning of English as a second language in Wales, helped by the knowledge that English occurs as L2 in many parts of the world and the points raised and suggestions made will be of interest and perhaps value elsewhere.

In their consideration of second language teaching the members of the Gittins Committee visited the Province of Quebec (Canada), Finland, Switzerland, Belgium and Denmark. Their general conclusion is pertinent:

Little of direct value to Wales resulted from these visits, partly because the circumstances were not often directly comparable to those in Wales and partly because the actual techniques of second language teaching observed were often traditional ones, which have not enjoyed any measure of success in this country (Gittins Report, 11. 9).

They also noted the success of Continental methods, particularly in the case of English as L2, and ascribed this not to technique so much as to motivation and community support for the language. The teaching of Irish in the Republic of Ireland provided a contrast in some ways, for, although it was very successfully taught as L2 in the elementary school, some 40 per cent of the time was given to it there, there was no continuation in the secondary school and less than full support for it in the community. They rightly emphasized the crucial role of speaking and hearing the language in L2 learning, and we have already seen that E2 in Wales has all the advantages, including motivation, operating increasingly in its favour as the pupil progresses through the school system.

In its specific consideration of E2 in Wales, the Gittins Report identified two possible approaches:

  (i) the experiences and interests of the child
 (ii) the linguistically based

and concluded that both were needed in that the children's learning should be centred on activity and interest, using properly selected, graded and prepared second language materials. It then drew attention to the need for research and development to produce the necessary schemes and material. Since 1967 little progress has been made in this field, though it is hoped that the Schools Council Project on 'English in Wales, 8–13', to start work in 1973, will achieve some at least of these goals. In the meantime we can explore the areas for further work and discussion, best done under appropriate headings.

1. Age of introduction

This seems the least controversial of aspects nowadays, although in the past it has caused endless arguments, mainly because so much emphasis was placed on reading and writing. No doubt the argument still rages in those areas with formal, traditional approaches. In Wales every W1 child comes to school with some English language background, even if only hearing English on television without understanding it, and it seems perverse to avoid all use of the language in school. The learning of E2 should start informally, therefore, in the infants school from the beginning, just as W2 may be introduced for the E1 child, if our aim is full bilingualism. The detail of how E2 is introduced and used at this stage must be decided by the teacher according to the ability and linguistic background of her children, but one envisages either an increasing use of the two languages side by side or times and activities nominated for English. Just as the infants school day is not rigidly time-tabled, so the language development must not be seen as rigidly structured at this age, but the teacher does need an awareness of all the factors involved, a point developed in Chapter 6. In most cases she will be assisted by the presence in the class of some E1 children or some E2 children with a basic command of the language, acquired before entering school. Certainly she will herself be bilingual and thus able to detect at once if the children are confused because she is pushing them too fast.

Implicit in the previous paragraph is the exclusively oral nature of E2 in the infants school. This should be continued into the junior school, but at some time during the four junior years E2 reading and writing must be introduced, as we have already seen in our discussion of the language medium. The child will learn to read and write in his native language, Welsh, and if his L2 reading and writing are introduced too soon he will become confused, much more so than when his L1 is purely oral and the L2 learning, equally oral, is begun. E2 reading and writing should be introduced when he is ready for them, therefore, but practical considerations dictate that if possible this should be during his junior school career, although there is a strong case for saying that if he cannot read or write in Welsh by the age of 11 + any insistence that he attempt to do so in English is not only a waste of time but positively harmful. Except in the very small junior schools which survive in Wales, we are concerned with groups or classes of children and must consider some kind of average performance. In these terms it is probably a sound guiding principle to suggest that E2 work in the first two years of the junior school should remain exclusively oral, leaving the introduction of reading and writing until the third year. 'When in doubt, delay' is good advice, for whereas the earlier start may do harm postponement has positive advantages, particularly in that later the children will learn more quickly and with less trouble. Indeed, many junior school headteachers have commented on the marked increase in native language literacy from the third to the fourth years, while it is worth noting that in W2 learning, where admittedly the pressures are different, there is a tendency for teachers more and more to concentrate solely on oral work, not only throughout the junior school but also in the first year or two of the secondary school. We need evidence of the effects of different practices, but in our concern to avoid the dangers of too early introduction of E2 reading and writing we must remember not to hold back the able, especially those who enter school with genuine bilingual proficiency.

2. Experiences and interests

The theoretical basis of this approach to mother-tongue development is best examined by reading Professor J. N. Britton's book,

53

Language and Learning. Language is vital to the total development of the child, for by it he handles and controls his environment, he uses it to consolidate and extend his experience in the great variety of situations which he increasingly meets as he grows up, including the many personal relationships in which he reacts by means of language. Over-simplified and crude as this brief statement is, it serves to indicate the kind of learning situation required. Language development will occur in any society without the intervention of the teacher, but this is not enough. The teacher has a positive role to play in ensuring that this development is encouraged and controlled, and above all that it does not stop short of the individual's full potential. His task is to provide the contexts which will stimulate the child's use of and response to language, at first in speech, later in writing, to give him the variety of activities and experiences which call forth the varieties of language appropriate to his stage of development, and to furnish both a measure of achievement and the necessary guidance and help. Personal expression will figure largely in the early stages, even in the kind of informational work done in the junior school in a project on environmental studies, for example, but impersonal speech and writing will come in due course when the pupil is ready. The demands on the teacher are great, of course, because he cannot work by rule of thumb but has to respond spontaneously in the immediate situation, becoming an active participant and partner rather than a remote controller and adjudicator. This outline of the mother-tongue approach, which has deliberately stopped short of the difficult question of structure, is particularly relevant to second-language learning and teaching in Wales.

Because of the linguistic background range described earlier, English will be taught as a first language to the majority. For the minority, W1 pupils, it will achieve almost the status of a native language by the time they leave school and will be taught as a first language during part at least of the secondary stage. These pupils need a command of the living language for everyday purposes comparable to that of native speakers, so that first language considerations must be taken into account, even though in the early stages there will be special E2 aspects. In short, the relationship between language and experience must be an integral part of E2 learning in this mixed situation, and the work in the classroom must in no sense be abstract or academic until the basic mastery has been acquired. At that stage there is an element of choice to be discussed later.

In the primary school, therefore, E2 learning will have a firm foundation in the experiences and interests of the children, running parallel to but not repeating the desirable first language work, consolidating and extending their experience and perhaps compensating for limited experience outside the school. It will be characterised by all those features of good primary practice found in England and the anglicized areas of Wales. There will be an emphasis, exclusive at first, on oral work, both talking and listening, and a constant effort to get the children to respond to all that goes on and formulate that response in English with developing assurance and subtlety. The teacher will read stories to the children, will encourage them to engage in dialogue and conversation, and will help individuals and groups to develop interests which will provide the essential contexts for language work. The skilful choice of activities and interests will enable the child to develop both expressive and practical uses of the language.

All this is fine and apparently straightforward until one asks the key questions. How does the teacher measure progress in order to know whether the methods adopted are successful or not? Progress in language learning, especially L1 and L2, is not a straight line and the concept should not be interpreted too narrowly, but even so some goal or goals in attainment should be considered, as was suggested earlier. Even more important and urgent in the classroom, how does the teacher decide which stories to read to children at the age of 8 or 9, and which situations should be devised in order to encourage language patterns and vocabulary appropriate to the stage of development? At the moment it is impossible or very difficult for the teacher to acquire the necessary knowledge, granted that it exists, a topic to be explored in Chapter 6. In practice he gains a certain expertise by trial and error, by intuition and by experience over a long period of time, a statement which is cold comfort to the young teacher and anathema to the teacher of any age who is not prepared to make the necessary effort. It is understandable in the circumstances if he abandons the approach based on experiences and interests, which he dismisses as woolly and lacking framework, and seeks the structure he needs by resorting to traditional, formal methods, using in all probability a course book designed for E1 children, which again may or may not be satisfactory for its original purpose. The next section will consider more satisfactory ways of answering the questions.

55

3. The linguistically-based approach

This depends in essence upon linguistic analysis of the target language, or in a bilingual situation of both the languages involved. Learning programmes are then prepared to deal systematically with the elements and aspects revealed by the analysis, emphasis being placed on a steady progression from the simple to the more complex and care being taken to cover all points by graded materials and language work. It also demands highly organized teaching methods, and is in general terms the most popular approach throughout the world for second language learning. Within the total area it is possible to distinguish two types: the first is older and based upon the traditional analysis of English, derived ultimately from Latin, while the second, more acceptable, uses modern ideas of the nature of the language, basing its schemes on the findings of linguistics during the last fifty years or so. The first is still found in English course books, though the contents are less rigorous, particularly in grammar, than they used to be. Textbooks or courses of the second kind are developing slowly but steadily in both first and second language teaching, in conventional and programmed learning approaches. Often, though not necessarily, linguistically-based courses of either kind use what has been called the brick-upon-brick approach in strict sequencing, requiring the pupil to master the various elements in turn and demonstrate his progress by the satisfactory completion of exercises which provide no or minimal context. The teacher of E2 in Wales may find this whole approach attractive, because it offers superficially satisfying answers to the questions asked above, in that its strict linguistic sequencing and frequent 'test' exercises offer both the desired framework and the measure of progress. But there is no such course available for E2 in Wales, so he is driven either to devise his own or to choose one prepared for other situations, usually E1 in England. Whichever choice he makes, inadequate or out-of-date knowledge about the nature of language is likely to lead him astray, with dull, sterile teaching as the consequence.

It is still a widely held belief that second language learning and teaching require the formal, highly structured approach described, however much mother-tongue work in schools may have moved away from it, though there are signs that ideas are changing, especially in recent work with immigrant children in England. If we accept the arguments of the previous section about experiences and interests, we can appreciate that E2 teaching in Wales does not need linguistic knowledge to produce formal, somewhat abstract courses with rigid structure, but it does need such knowledge to inform its methods and materials in the way exemplified for E1 by *Breakthrough to Literacy* and *Language in Use*. We do not require linguistic knowledge to provide the content of courses for pupils, though the role and nature of language study is a controversial aspect covered in Chapter 5, but rather we must have it to give us sound information about language and languages so that we may select and grade materials, devise the best methods and handle language skilfully in the classroom. (For a further discussion of these aspects, the reader should consult B. Harrison's book in this series, *English as a Second and Foreign Language*.)

As far as E2 in Wales is concerned the work remains to be done, although the necessary body of knowledge is steadily accumulating. Nor is it a task for individual teachers, hard-pressed as they are, but rather for a combined operation by groups of teachers, working as separate groups but also co-operating with each other, who can call upon expert advice and information when needed, the whole co-ordinated by a team such as that in a typical Schools Council Research and Development Project. The requirements are gradually becoming clear. The teachers bring their training, experience and knowledge of children to the development of E2 methods and materials. What do they ask of the linguist?

First and foremost they require a descriptive analysis of each of the two languages, in this case Welsh and English, and then definition of the areas of interference between them, in this case again the particular problems likely to be encountered by the W1 learner of English. These are in themselves tall orders, and it is not practicable to wait for their completion before proceeding with development. We must use what is available and what can be achieved in the short term, modifying later in the light of further knowledge. Thus the standard way of examining areas of interference between languages is by the linguistic technique known as contrastive analysis, but this is a lengthy process and demands an expertise which is rare, i.e. the number of Welsh-speaking linguists capable of carrying it out is very small indeed. The alternative is error analysis, by which W1 children of various age-groups are given English attainment tests and the results are analysed to determine those points which do in fact cause them trouble. This is obviously more economical and of more direct help, but the linguist still has an important albeit more limited role to play, for his task becomes that of deciding initially the likely areas that should be covered by the tests and of distinguishing subsequently between genuine interference effects and difficulties likely to be faced by all learners of English.

This kind of fundamental, analytical knowledge of the languages is not all that is needed, however, because of the bilingual's peculiar situation. He is inevitably more aware of language in his environment, more likely to identify language and culture, more liable to experience the complications of language usage, because he is operating in both Welsh and English, and at least initially and probably for some years at a higher level in one than in the other. For this reason there is a case to be made for the earlier introduction in E2 of conscious language study, earlier, that is, than would be considered desirable in E1. The point also emphasizes the need to take into account those psychological and social aspects of language which have received inadequate attention in the past and which embrace not only the nature but also the function of language in the total context of society. If the bilingual is eventually to approach or achieve E1 proficiency although he is E2 initially, he must be well versed in the varieties of English and this must be allowed for in the early stages of learning. To begin with he will be restricted to one variety of English, not, we trust, the old-fashioned 'correct' English but rather an educated, conversational, idiomatic English which will enable him later to extend his range rapidly under guidance in school and with the supporting background outside, moving easily from the spoken to the written in due course. These aspects will be covered more fully in Chapter 5 and, from the point of view of the teacher, in Chapter 6, but it is important to note them here to indicate the kind of linguistic knowledge which should inform E2 methods and materials.

The difference between using linguistic knowledge to structure a rigidly sequential course based mainly on the acquisition of the elements of the language and the use of similar knowledge to provide a framework of a much looser kind, giving many alternative choices for the teacher, is a vital one, and indicates the proper amalgam of approaches, based both on the children's experiences and interests and on language study.

4. Oracy

It would not be appropriate here to justify the importance of oral work in mother-tongue learning. Those interested but unconvinced or wishing to know more should study the work of Dr Andrew Wilkinson and various publications of the National Association for the Teaching of English, such as *Children Using Language*.

In a bilingual situation certain of the arguments take on an added significance, for any realistic policy of bilingual education must allow for the fact that the majority of bilinguals will use one of their two languages, usually the L2, mainly in its spoken forms. Certain qualifications must be borne in mind, though; until very recently in Wales, for example, some official business could be conducted only in English, because bilingual government forms were not printed. Apart from causing resentment, an important consideration, this meant that bilinguals whose first language was Welsh had to achieve basic literacy in English. Some bilinguals, of course, will enter professions in which literacy in both languages is essential, as in some academic circles or parts of the civil service. For these and other reasons, an emphasis on oracy as a prime objective must not lead to a neglect of reading and writing in the L2. We should be more discriminating in our approach to second language teaching, realizing that less academic pupils whose literacy in their L1 is limited will be better served by an attempt to improve their L2 oral proficiency than by time wasted on L2 reading and writing.

Other factors have already been mentioned, and it is not necessary to repeat them here. The conclusion is that E2 learning should begin in the infants school and that it should remain an entirely oral activity until the later junior stages, or the early secondary years for weaker pupils.

5. The relationship between E2 and E1

It was established in Chapter 2 that there is a wide range of linguistic background amongst pupils in the schools of Wales. Even in the Welsh-speaking areas it is unusual to find a class without some E1 children, many classes elsewhere are truly mixed in this respect, and the majority of schools in the principality are predominantly E1. Geographically schools of different language backgrounds may be close to each other. In any mixed bilingual situation of this kind L2 methods must not be developed in isolation from L1 methods and materials, though equally the differences must not be ignored. The point is specially important in the type of situation used as the basis for this whole discussion, because minority-language speakers must develop native language proficiency if possible in the world language. As we have seen, this means that at some later stage of their L2 learning L1 methods and materials will be adopted and the L2 approach gradually abandoned, so in order to make this as smooth and continuous a process as possible the L2 approach used in the early stages should recognize and use where appropriate the principles of the L1 approach. Much will depend on the nature of the two languages involved.

How, then, does this help us in our consideration of E2 learning and teaching? What guide-lines can we discover by an examination of E1 practice in England and Wales? Unfortunately the guiding principles may be clear in theory but confused in practice, for during the last fifteen to twenty years many changes in the teaching of English as a mother-tongue have been recommended and have in fact taken place, though not evenly. There has been a commendable reaction against formal methods and the wholesale use of language exercises, in favour of more creative work and greater freedom for the pupil. As a consequence, it is impossible to generalize about E1 teaching practice in the schools of Wales at present, because, as in England, the whole range from the traditional, formal class method to the progressive, informal group or individual approach can be observed, sometimes within the same school, and certainly within the same area. What is relevant here is that many teachers are aware of new methods and willing to adopt them, but a feeling of doubt and limited understanding leads them to seek more guidance and explanation than has been traditionally provided. The complications of language in a bilingual community add to the confusion experienced by some teachers in a monoglot situation, for it is easy to misunderstand new ideas or to transfer them from one language to another without fully grasping the implications.

An examination of three key examples is worthwhile in order to clarify the point and to link with earlier ideas in building up the progression from E2 to E1 for the W1 pupil. One most important area is children's expression, both oral and written. In recent years it has been fashionable to urge great attention to this, and we are familiar with books on creative, personal or intensive writing and their equivalents for oral work, so much so that we may come to distrust the whole affair and dismiss personal expression as of little value, or at least over-rated. The vital part played by it in children's language development cannot be dismissed, of course, and there is no need to labour its importance for both first and second language learning. What is of more concern is what has happened in practice in some cases, for 'expression' has been taken by some as the *only* road to salvation, so that no other work in English is attempted. In other cases, teachers have believed that it does not matter what the children say or write as long as they express themselves, and that critical comment or assessment can do nothing but harm. Others again have misunderstood the pleas for perspective in looking at children's pronunciation, syntax, spelling and punctuation, and have stated that these aspects do not matter and must not be corrected. In the past children were perhaps not stimulated sufficiently to express themselves; now there is a danger that they will be over-stimulated and that the focus of attention will move from the child's experience and consequent expression to the teacher's ingenuity in devising a wide variety of sensory stimuli. It is easy to exaggerate the weaknesses and misunderstandings, but false notions can cause teachers to ignore or treat superficially important aspects of language work. Without doubt personal expression, at first oral, later oral and written, must be one of the threads which link L2 and L1 learning and teaching.

False notions and a plentiful supply of poor textbooks, in some cases devised for E1 but used with E2 pupils, have also caused confusion in the minds of teachers about comprehension work, often dismissed as futile. So many comprehension exercises offered are indeed sterile, being based on very short, worthless passages and concerning themselves solely with the factual content and the vocabulary. But inadequacy of the instruments must not cause neglect of this equally important aspect of language development. It is vital that children should be trained to respond as fully as possible to the language usage of others, in both speech and writing, and they should be given every opportunity of developing their understanding of the literal meaning and the emotional content of what they read and hear. It may well be that this is best done incidentally, for certainly a rich language experience in the classroom provides all the material desirable, but there is a risk that the overworked teacher may pay less than sufficient attention to reading comprehension, in contrast to oral comprehension, where failure to understand is usually immediately obvious. There is also, naturally enough, a tendency to concentrate on literal meaning at the expense of those subtleties of language such as tone and intention which become increasingly important as the child grows older. Regular and systematic comprehension work is essential for the E2 learner, another linking thread, and it must cover the varieties of English which he needs to master if he is to become fully bilingual.

The third area has been deliberately chosen to raise the question of the relationship between language and literature, so often artificially divorced in schools. Literature is a major aspect of language usage in many languages, and as such merits the attention which it has received and is receiving. Indeed, there are some who suggest that literature provides all the material that is properly needed for language work in schools, and they will have nothing or little to do with other approaches to language, but this attitude ignores so many uses of language close to the pupils' immediate experience and is unnecessarily confining. On the other hand, in the Welsh and similar situations language looms large and it is only too easy to concentrate on it. It is essential that children should read as widely as possibly in their first language, that they should be helped to respond as fully as they can to what they read, and that they should be accustomed to listening to stories and poems read to them by the teacher. The emphasis throughout must be on enjoyment if we wish them to see reading as one worthwhile way of spending time as they grow older and encounter competing demands on their leisure hours. It is important in the primary school, therefore, to surround them with books, readily accessible and attractive to look at and handle, and to show them that poetry is fun, especially when spoken aloud, not a subject for dissection, line by line, word by word. In the secondary school this general emphasis on enjoyment and response must continue, though the more academic classes will be moving steadily towards criticism in the true sense. The relationship between E1 and E2 literature work now becomes clear, for if the teacher reads to the children from the beginning of E2 and if their experience of Welsh literature is as outlined above, there are no problems of transition when they start reading in English at a later stage, so that their study of Welsh and English literature will proceed side by side. Where there is no literature in the native, minority language the problems are very different and solutions can be sought only in the light of local conditions.

One other feature of literature work should be mentioned. Although it acts in favour of the W1 pupil's English language development, it is unfortunate that in the early secondary years he will tend to turn more and more to English books, simply because there are so many interesting and suitable ones available, in contrast to the limited amount of Welsh reading which is attractive to the 12- to 14-year-old. Efforts are being made to remedy this, but they are not likely to make much impact in the short term. Similarly, it is sensible to suggest that because the literature chosen should be not only within the pupil's capability but also linked to his experience and interests Anglo-Welsh literature should figure prominently for the E2 learner. This cultural base can and should be used in the fourth and fifth years of the secondary school, but below that stage the same practical problem is encountered: there is very little suitable Anglo-Welsh literature, the problem becoming more acute as one moves down the age-range.

In this field as in others so many factors operate to the advantage of the world language in a situation like that of Wales that special measures are needed to preserve and extend the minority language. We are not concerned here with whether these special measures are justified; it is assumed that they are, and that one task of the educational system is to safeguard the interests of the speakers of the minority language, not least by preparing and developing second language methods and materials.

6. Summary and conclusions

When the members of the Gittins Committee identified the two approaches to E2, that based on experiences and interests and the linguistically-based, they also suggested that both were needed, not separately but fused. We can now see that the way to achieve this fusion is the development of a language-based course for E1 and E2, with literature as one major language area. Desirable in itself, this approach is essential for E2 language development as outlined and its later merging with E1 methods.

It is easy to write this, but the work remains to be done. The kind of course envisaged would place the emphasis on language in action, on a series of situations and contexts designed to exercise in a real way the pupils' use of and response to language. The teacher's task would not simply be the creation of the learning environment, important though this is, but by participation, comment, suggestion and clarification the active encouragement of development. We have some knowledge, mostly empirical, of how to decide which situations and stimuli are appropriate for the different ages, but we need much more if we are to grade our materials as we should like. From linguists and educationalists we need more information about the varieties of speech and writing, about ways of stimulating response and expression, about how we can judge the language difficulty of works of literature, about how to handle the language we actually get in the classroom. In short, we require more knowledge about the nature and function of language and about the language development of children. But we have enough for us to start, and we are constantly gaining more, so that we can refine as we proceed.

The structure provided in this way should not be seen as a rigid framework, strictly sequential, for either E1 or E2. It is not of the kind which demands mastery of one construction before another is tackled, for first and second language learning in a bilingual community is not an isolated, artificial activity whereby we hope the pupil will grasp one element once and for all and subsequently need only 'revision'. Rather we seek his increasing command of the infinite variety possible, and our grading is intended to ensure that he progresses from the easier to the more difficult context, not encountering abstract argument before he can cope with it, to take an obvious example. Even so, in similar situations one group will reveal a more sophisticated language usage than another of the same age and ability, and the same group will vary in level from day to day or hour to hour. Development is not in a straight line, so our course involves constant repetition of similar language demands, with increasing refinement over a period of a term or a year, and our grading consists of extending the range step by step as far as the ability of the pupil permits. Linguistic knowledge enables us to make judgments both in preparation and in the classroom, but it is not part of the course for the pupil in any direct sense and certainly not in any sense in the early stages. In a bilingual community it also enables us to take into account interference effects and other special features referred to earlier.

Within this loose framework there will doubtless be a need from time to time for concentrated attention on individual aspects of language usage which are causing trouble, perhaps a construction which cannot be properly mastered, perhaps a distinction between the formal and casual styles the lack of which is responsible for practical problems in school. These are matters for the teacher to decide, and it is to be hoped that the explanation offered will allay the fears of those English teachers who regard any attempt to impose structure on the syllabus as anathema, as inevitably a return to the dark ages. Although it was convenient in the last section to isolate certain aspects of English work for brief comment, it must be realized that one present weakness in the teaching of E1 is the fragmentation which has resulted from the many rival claims made in recent years, and this has affected E2 teaching, where an absence of structure can be even less easily tolerated. Nor must what has been said be interpreted as a desire to impose one unified system of teaching and set of materials. The principles involved are vital, but it is also vital to maintain the freedom of the individual teacher to choose his methods and materials for himself, to suit his particular pupils and circumstances; it is also necessary to help him to make an informed choice and to have access to the best practice of others. The type of system required is elastic, embodying the linguistic and pedagogic knowledge not readily available to the individual and providing a graded scheme of teaching materials sufficient in scope at each level for choices to be made.

Other important points made about E2 methods and materials in Wales, though many have a wider application, include:

(a) There should be an emphasis throughout on oracy. Command of the spoken language should have priority until E1 methods are adopted, when it assumes equal importance with command of the written forms.

(b) E2 work should begin in the infants school and become systematic in the junior school.

(c) Reading and writing should not be introduced until they are firmly established in the first language. For most this means in the third or fourth year of the junior school.

(d) There should be a smooth, gradual transition from the E2 to the E1 approach, depending on the pupils' progress. For the majority it should take place during the first two years of the secondary stage. E2 considerations have generally been ignored too soon.

(e) There must be greater flexibility in the treatment of pupils of varying ability, especially modifications in aims, emphases and rates for the academically weaker.

(f) The approach is not only bilingual, it is also bi-cultural. This must be borne in mind all the time, but particularly in the choice of literature.

(g) The choice of language medium for teaching has an important effect on language learning in a bilingual community.

(h) The factors in the total environment operate in favour of E2. Contrast the position of W2.

(i) The social context of language is even more important in a bilingual community than elsewhere. An orderly, progressive course is best based on language development. When these two points are considered together, the role of language study is seen as crucial and will be defined and explored in the next chapter.

5 Studying language in the classroom

It became clear in the last chapter that there are rival claims for different approaches to the teaching and learning of English, and that these complications are added to those inherent in a bilingual community which has English as one of its two languages. Argument rages, fiercely at times, over the respective merits of formal and informal methods, of the traditional and the progressive approaches, of the creative and the logical, of language-based and literature-based courses, and of the structural and experiential schemes. These labels represent extreme positions and it is undoubtedly true that most teachers are somewhere in between the furthest points on the scale from formal to informal, but there is a genuine conflict of opinion and emphasis which is reflected in a wide range of practice in the classroom. By selecting as an example one area of controversy, that between formal and informal, we can see that the different conflicts are variations on a theme, which may be over-simplified as the contrast between rigidity and flexibility, or structural and intuitive approaches, though this does not apply to the distinction between language and literature as the basis of the syllabus, for whichever is chosen either of the two methods may be adopted.

Far too often positions are taken up which advocate nothing but good in the preferred approach and nothing but evil in the rejected one, without any recognition of the possibility of compromise, or of synthesizing the best in each. The solution offered in Chapter 4 is an attempt to achieve this synthesis, albeit it sees language as providing the desirable but not rigid framework. Within this structure many different methods may be used, whether we are considering E1 or E2, but there is one particular area of controversy which runs as a common thread through all the arguments referred to and which has a special significance in a bilingual situation: the precise relationship between language study and language development.

The questions are obvious. Although the teacher clearly needs to know as much about language as possible, does the pupil also need a conscious knowledge of how the language works? If so, what kind of knowledge does he need? Does he, for example, need to know the grammar or patterns of the language, or is it more valuable for him to study the social aspects? At what age should such a study begin, if at all? Is it suitable only for the more able pupils? What relative importance should be attached to study of the language as opposed to practice in its use and response to it? The reader can surely add further questions of his own.

Before attempting to answer these questions, however, we must define terms, for 'language study' is used with many different meanings, ranging from linguistics in the professional sense at one end of the scale to any effort by a teacher to get a child to choose a better word in a certain context at the other. It is helpful to use the term 'studying language' when we are thinking of schools and teaching, and to restrict its meaning to studying the patterns of a natural language explicitly with the object of increasing pupils' command of a language. It occurs in any teaching or learning situation in which the pupil is asked to formulate in explicit terms knowledge about language, whether this formulation is based on his own observation (as we should in general prefer) or is a repetition of what he has been told. Studying language in this way includes both the complex, such as a four-year course in traditional grammar, and the simple or limited, such as the study by a class of the speech habits of its teachers. To be fair, the complex example might equally well be the study over a long period of time of different registers, and the simple one an examination of the accusative case in English. Which of the two approaches contained in the examples is more relevant to the pupil's language learning will be our main concern later in this chapter.

In contrast to studying language is what we may call 'working with language'. This covers any teaching or learning situation in which the pupil is *not* asked to formulate in explicit terms knowledge about language, and it is part of the commerce of daily life in the classroom. The awareness of language remains implicit, intuitive, and the teacher concentrates on improving the pupil's use of and response to the language without making him conscious of the relevant information about the nature and function of the

68

language. It covers so much, from the teacher's helping the child to find the right 'name' for an object or happening in the infants school to a discussion of the most effective sentence construction in a secondary school composition, from a joint effort to gain precision of expression in the response to a poem in the junior school to a sixth-form discussion of the subtleties of literature. Its aim is to seek the right or better word or phrase and not to ask the pupil to explain why it is right or better, though if he should ask us we should explain if possible within the limits of his understanding.

The assistance and guidance provided in this way is an intrinsic and very important part of the mother-tongue teacher's task, but we hope that it is not restricted to lessons labelled English or Welsh, for it should occur whenever the pupil is expressing himself or comprehending others, whatever the subject-matter or the task in hand. All teachers should be conscious of the need to work with language, though in most lessons it will arise incidentally, whereas in language teaching it is an essential part of the scheme and the teacher devises tasks and provides material, spoken and written, with language work very much in mind. It is true that children's language development will take place in any society without the intervention of the teacher, and some teachers see their function as nurturing the natural growth without interference. But this is not enough, because the teacher has a responsibility to ensure by every means available that the child's command of language develops as rapidly and as far as possible, taking into account the other agencies, notably the home and the local environment, which in most cases will assist the process but which sometimes prove a handicap. As has been said, working with language covers a wide range of complexity and formality, but in its simplest form it should be part of the daily routine from the beginning of the infants school. Getting children to talk about the previous day's happenings, often called the diary, and respond to questions and comments is an example, though often at this stage language work will be incidental to physical activities of many varied kinds. As the child progresses from the infants to the junior to the secondary school, working with language should become gradually more and more explicit, but it is always distinguished from studying language by its concern with the instinctive, intuitive development of control of language and by an absence of any attempt to teach the child *about* the language, to make explicit what is happening when he handles the language.

Working with language makes great demands on a teacher's skill and knowledge, because it is part of a constant flow and he does not know which aspect or which point of detail is going to arise next. He can control events to a certain extent, by creating situations and selecting materials, but he cannot ultimately determine in advance the precise forms of the language which will occur, unless his approach is so rigid that he insists on one correct version or teaches rules imposed on the living language. There will be an examination of the teacher's needs in Chapter 6, but the intention here is to emphasize the difficulty of his task even in a monolingual situation. It would not be true to suggest that in a bilingual community the demands and difficulties are twice as great, but without doubt there are added problems. Ideally the teacher should be not only fluent in both languages but should also have considerable knowledge about them and the areas of possible interference between them. To this must be added a knowledge of children and the language learning process, both first and second language. When we realize that in many bilingual communities there are not enough fluent speakers of the two languages involved, especially where one is a minority language, to fill all teaching posts in bilingual schools, we can appreciate the problem of meeting the requirements of skill and knowledge, and the need to train bilingual teachers initially and in-service. More than this, they should have every assistance from educational agencies outside the school, because some of their most difficult problems are caused by the very nature of the bilingual community. An obvious and very serious example is provided by the fact that in some Welsh-speaking areas of Wales an increasing number of children are entering school without a first language in any proper sense. Their Welsh and their English are so poor and adulterated that they have two second languages and are likely to be severely handicapped throughout their school careers. Another example is the teacher's need to be able to switch the language medium and to know when to do this and when not.

Much more could be written about this, but the point has been made that teachers require Language Study, as defined by Peter Doughty in *Language Study, the Teacher and the Learner*, as part of their professional equipment and that in bilingual communities the knowledge of language and languages must be both wider and deeper. To what extent is studying language in the sense defined desirable or necessary for the pupil? It is clear that the distinction between working with language and studying language is a

70

working one. There are no watertight compartments, for any teacher at any time may make explicit a language point in answer to a question or because he thinks it aids expression or response. But such incidental or casual study of language is a far cry from a systematic attempt to give pupils an understanding of how a language works or how language works by giving specific attention to the subject over a period of time, though not, we hope, one lesson a week for five years, as with the traditional secondary approach to grammar.

The language development of the pupil must be the criterion for schools and we are learning more all the time about the kind of language exploration, embracing both working with and studying, which promotes this development. We still know comparatively little about the impact of studying language and the proper relationship between it and language development, although we have come to realize that traditional methods such as grammar and language exercises dealing with words out of context do not increase a pupil's sensitivity to language or his command in general, even though they may do little harm to the able. A rejection of misguided methods based on a false view of language should not lead us to a total abandonment of studying language, a position reached by many teachers, but rather to a consideration of alternative approaches which may be more relevant to the pupil's needs. At the appropriate stage an awareness of how language works will give him an increased sensitivity in his understanding and use of it and studying language becomes an integral and important part of working with language. The traditional analytical approach does not have this effect on the vast majority of pupils, and certainly not on the less able, who are simply baffled, but other methods to be discussed later are suitable for all levels of ability.

Studying language in the sense defined earlier has this important part to play in the development of all pupils, but it has special relevance to the bilingual's situation for two reasons. The first is that he is much more aware from an early age of the language environment, he cannot but notice that there are two languages even if he uses only one, that some people use one and others both, that the language used varies from situation to situation, and so on. Initially this awareness will not be conscious, though at school he will encounter problems of equivalence and perhaps status, but as he grows up he will inevitably become conscious of many of the factors involved, he will adopt attitudes and express views on the language aspects of life in a bilingual community, either privately or in the political arena. It is important, therefore, that his views and actions should be firmly based on a proper understanding of the nature and function of language, for though this is unlikely to eliminate prejudice and myth entirely it will in general lead to a more rational and sympathetic approach. Looking at this point from another angle, we can say that the teacher should take advantage of the bilingual's natural interest in language and its social context. The second reason concerns the majority of bilinguals who do not enter school with a command of both languages and who consequently learn one as a second language. At some stage a deliberate discussion which makes the similarities and differences between the two languages explicit and consciously grasped will assist development in both.

'At some stage' and the earlier 'at the appropriate stage' draw attention to the need to examine the role and nature of studying language in greater depth. In order to do this we shall look at English in Wales, a particular situation, for reasons given in the previous chapter on language teaching methods, bearing in mind that conclusions of wider application may be drawn. For monoglot pupils in anglicized areas it is probably right to suggest that there should be no systematic study of language during the primary school stage. The emphasis throughout this period up to the age of 11 should be on working with language, but it is not easy, and may be foolhardy, to make categorical statements in this field and we must recognize the casual, isolated study of language mentioned above and perhaps the value of short-term and simple conscious exploration in the last year of the junior school when many children develop a liking for playing with words. This is a matter for the teacher's judgment, but studying language should not be considered for pupils who are struggling with basic literacy, nor should it ever be so extensive as to deprive any pupil of the rich language experience vital at the junior stage. For reasons already suggested, E2 pupils and E1 pupils in Welsh-speaking areas are likely to benefit from the introduction of some study of language in the primary stage, particularly in the last two years of the junior school. It should be very simple and should arise from the pupil's working with language, directly linked to his expression and comprehension. When the E2 pupil starts reading and writing in English it is natural and helpful to explain to him the different spelling systems of the two languages, something which will have to be repeated from time to time in most cases, and this is an example of the desirable approach. Cross-reference between the two languages is the key to this simple study of language and it cannot be emphasized enough that it should be related to work with language and experience and should not be abstract or analytical in the grammatical sense.

In the secondary school studying language should play an increasingly important part without sacrificing the essential emphasis on working with language, the use of and response to language. Just as the pupil's power of abstract argument develops during this period, so should his awareness of the nature and function of language become steadily more conscious, so that he may fully appreciate the subtleties of literature on the one hand and the manipulations of advertisers on the other. How far he goes and how deeply he penetrates will depend as in any other sphere on his ability, but the right kind of study, closely related to language development, is beneficial for all levels of ability and is consequently suitable for mixed-ability groupings. It is also appropriate for groups of mixed linguistic background, for there is a wider spread of language experience to draw upon in these classes. At the secondary stage the E2 pupil is moving towards E1 proficiency, attitudes and approaches, so it is possible to discuss studying language during this period for all pupils in Welsh schools without forgetting the differences of linguistic background represented in many classes. Because language is a common talking-point and some aspect of it features regularly in newspapers, it is even easier to make studying language 'real' in a bilingual community than in a monoglot.

Studying language, properly structured and systematic, has a contribution to make in the secondary school, but the nature of the study is crucial. It cannot assist language development if it is highly abstract, remote from the living language or too difficult for the pupils to master. By these standards traditional grammar and language exercises typified by 'correction of sentences' must be rejected, and have been by very many teachers. Instead there should be a concentration on the varieties of language encountered by the pupil and an attempt to extend his language experience in this conscious way as well as in his intuitive working with language. Any examination of the patterns of the language should have significance and relevance for him at his stage of development, but the primary concern should be the study of how language functions in personal relationships and in wider social contexts. The weakest pupil can contribute something, for even if he cannot read he can talk and listen, a reminder that we are concerned equally with the oral and the written. The usual but not immutable method should be a preliminary, fairly brief discussion of the topic, which may have arisen from the group's language work or may have been introduced by the teacher, followed by a period of perhaps a week during which members of the group carry out 'research' by collecting examples from sources such as literature, home, newspapers, radio, television and other lessons as appropriate. Then these are collected and collated, and conclusions drawn, preferably by the pupils but prompted if necessary by the teacher. This basic pattern is capable of considerable variation, but the important features are the active participation of the pupils as opposed to their passive reception of knowledge imparted by the teacher, and the fact that examples of living language are used in contrast to carefully selected 'specimens' presented by the teacher. The time devoted to a topic may also vary, as may the number covered in a year, to suit its importance, or the value attached to studying language by the teacher, or the stage of development of the pupils. Material collected in this way by bilingual pupils will embrace many topics of immediate concern, such as the reasons for the appearance in some varieties of Welsh of many English words and the absence of Welsh words from the English used in the same community. This brief outline is intended to establish certain principles before looking at content in what is bound to be a selective way.

It is most important that all the study should be based on the methods and findings of modern linguistics, and particularly on that branch known as institutional linguistics, for our aim is to give our pupils an understanding of language usage in society, covering as many aspects as possible and not confining ourselves to the written forms of literature. This is an essential secondary school approach in any society, but its value is especially felt in bilingual communities. For instance, a study of language variations in social groupings in England will be concerned with features of English peculiar to the different groups; in a bilingual area of Wales the study would involve varieties of English *and* varieties of Welsh, as well as consideration of factors affecting the choice as to which of the two languages should be used by a group or on a specific occasion. If we realize that in a unilingual society it is not possible to cover all the desirable aspects of studying language in a secondary school course, we can readily appreciate the bilingual teacher's need to be selective and to

74

choose those areas of special relevance to his pupils' present and future lives. A wealth of material and methods is thus indicated as necessary so that the teacher may have this freedom of choice.

Having realized the futility of traditional grammar and course-book teaching, many individuals and groups of teachers have been experimenting with new approaches to secondary school language study for some twenty years, but most of this work has been extremely limited and known to others outside the particular school only by accident. Some of the work, too, was bound to be incomplete and therefore restricted in value simply because no complete, new grammar of English was available, and much of the exploration had a grammatical bias. The first large-scale production in this field came from the Schools Council Programme in Linguistics and English Teaching in 1971, made possible by the joint efforts over a period of years of a research and development team. *Language in Use* meets two fundamental requirements: it is informed by sound linguistic knowledge and it is the result of extensive field work in schools and colleges. It has other advantages as well, in that it can be used over a wide range of age and ability, from the later years of the Junior School, through the Secondary School, to Colleges of Further and Higher Education. It is also valuable for in-service courses for teachers and other adults whost job requires an awareness of language in action. This point has particular importance in a bilingual community where students, even in the same class or group, may well be at widely different levels of proficiency in English and the teachers need schemes and materials which may be dealt with either simply or more extensively and penetratingly. All the suggestions are not suitable for the younger groups, whether measured chronologically or by years as an English learner, but many of them are.

The arrangement of the material provides both guidance and freedom. Each unit in the scheme can be dealt with briefly or over a longer period of study. Presented in a loose-leaf binding, the units are grouped on the basis of linked relevance, but the individual teacher is free to group them differently (some alternatives are suggested) to suit local circumstances, wherever and whatever these may be. The materials and methods are designed for studying the English language, but in principle and often in detail they can be readily adapted for the study of other languages and for a contrastive study of two languages in the schools and colleges of a bilingual community. It would be out of place here to continue in this vein, but the reader should examine *Language in Use* and the supporting book, *Exploring Language*, for himself, with his own needs and problems in mind.

Some selective examination of the methods and content will be helpful at this stage, however, in order to establish its suitability for the E1 pupil or student *and* the E2 learner whose instinctive, intuitive awareness of the ways in which the English language works will be less and who is assisted in his usage by being made conscious of the intricacies, once he has achieved basic proficiency. The work 'does not require pupils to make detailed and explicit analytical statements', though these could be covered if desired, but it is concerned with the relationship between pupils and their language—and we can add for the bilinguals 'their languages'. 'This relationship has two major aspects: what pupils should know about the nature and function of language and how they can extend their command of their own language in both speaking and writing' (page 8). In this way the scheme combines working with language and studying language as defined earlier in this chapter, often in the same unit. Thus B5 'Front page' involves both study of newspapers and an attempt to produce original work, while sometimes the process is reversed, as in E8 'Fiction and reality', which starts by asking the class to write short stories of a particular kind.

Language in Use concentrates on that aspect which is of special concern in a bilingual community, language as human behaviour, and divides the whole into three parts which indicate relevance to all situations: I Language—its nature and function, II Language and individual man, III Language and social man. Within each part the units are arranged in themes, ten in all; for example, part III covers language in individual relationships, language in social relationships and language in social organizations. Remember that any individual teacher can use the groupings suggested by the authors or can devise his own scheme which may take units from any or all of the themes and combine them to produce a course tailor-made for his own pupils and local circumstances.

A closer look at some of the themes suggests how this adaptation can be carried out in a bilingual situation and also illustrates many of the points already made. The second theme in Part I is called 'Using language expressively' and is a good example of combining working with and studying language in exploring language to develop pupils' awareness of how language may be used in ways which may seem but are not purely informative, in order that their own response to such language and use of it

76

themselves may become more sensitive and effective. As one would expect, the topics covered in this theme include advertising, persuasion, and formal and informal, but one, unit B6 'Bias', is particularly well suited for an exploration of the different positions taken up in a bilingual community as revealed by the language used. A topical example in Wales at the moment is the campaign led by the Welsh Language Society to persuade all authorities to make their road-signs bilingual. Activities have included the uprooting of signs and the obliteration with paint of English-only signs, so naturally there have been several court cases. A bilingual class in Wales could easily collect reports of such a case from both Welsh and English papers, and then examine the ways in which the information given is selected in accordance with the paper's attitude to the Welsh language, or to the Society, or to 'illegal activities in support of a worthy cause', or to the courts, and so on. A lesson or series of lessons like this would arouse strong emotion, of course, but the skilful teacher could use this in itself to feed further discussion of language in action in similar contexts. The possibilities are many and need not be spelt out, though it is worth noting that this kind of work is self-generating in the sense that each exploration opens up other avenues for further examination, partly because the pupils can see the relevance and importance of language work in their own social context and are therefore involved, putting forward suggestions for new areas of study all the time. It cannot be said often enough that in a bilingual society such work in schools will not solve the social problems, but that the greater understanding it gives of language complications will in time lead towards solutions where these are possible.

The value of a theme such as F, 'Language and culture', can be immediately appreciated against this background. The bilingual's two languages give him access, consciously or unconsciously, to two cultures, which may in general be very similar or very different, though however similar they may be there will be differences which in many cases will cause conflicts of loyalties. Learning a language involves acquiring the values and attitudes of the community using the language, learning two languages which have or gain equal or near-equal status in the individual's life presents him with many moments of choice or confusion. In minority-language communities the sense of belonging is usually very strong, but career prospects and the chance to lead a fuller life so often lie with the world language. The social problems become enormous, as is witnessed by the declining population in many predominantly Welsh-speaking areas of Wales, not in itself a result of language factors alone but of economic and rural/urban distinctions which cause difficulties in other societies and which in a bilingual country can cause the decay of a community and the consequent gradual disappearance of a minority language. By working in schools to increase understanding of all that is involved we can at least hope for informed decisions at all levels. The units of theme F, then, provide a framework for the study of community values and attitudes, seen in Chapter 2 to be so important in Wales, by a conscious comparison of the Welsh and English cultures and an examination of misconceptions which exist and thrive.

We can start in a simple way with F2, for the distinctions between 'man's job' and 'woman's work' are deeply rooted in Welsh life, both inside and outside the home. Changes are occurring, but are these as rapid as in English areas or England? Do you notice any difference from area to area in the wording of the situations vacant column of local newspapers? Notice that the teacher must supply outside reference from experience, literature, newspapers and magazines, though he may be assisted by 'foreigners' in his class. 'Attitudes from fiction', F5, is a rich vein to explore, for the typical representation of the Welsh man or woman in English fiction, including television, is so stereotyped and limited to a few salient features which contrast strongly with reality that even weaker pupils can find plenty to observe and discuss. The work of this unit combines well with F6, 'National characteristics', in an extended exploration of stereotypes. Many Welshmen regard the English, for example, as snobbish, and the whole area is so fraught with emotion that the Attitudes Project had to abandon its attempt to measure by a semantic differential test attitudes towards people (Welsh and English) as well as towards the two languages because so much heat was engendered in the schools. What is inappropriate and perhaps misleading in a large-scale survey is often well suited to a controlled class-room discussion in which everyone is quickly and deeply interested.

F10 gives an opportunity to examine and discuss regional speech, both idiom and accent, a topic which again distinguishes the values and attitudes of different sections in a bilingual community such as Wales. With younger pupils in the secondary school the work can be restricted to noting the differences between the English accent and idiom of north and south Wales, of rural, urban and city communities; and comparing them with other regional speech throughout the English-speaking world, with the tapes and records now available. Older pupils can use this study as a basis for discussion of whether the differences in English between north and south Wales are parallel to differences in the Welsh of the two areas, or a consideration of the influence of the Liverpool accent on certain areas of north Wales. All such observation and drawing of conclusions leads to a greater awareness of the intimate relationship between language and community in a complex bilingual situation. A final example from the same theme is of particular relevance to the E2 learner, whose English may well be of one kind which is too formal for many occasions. Whether this restriction is the result of too 'academic' an approach in the early stages, or whether the lack of flexibility is caused by uncertain command of the language, the secondary pupil will benefit from a deliberate study of notions of 'correctness', linked with A3 ('Judging your audience'). Indeed, this is one good starting point for the whole of the work under consideration in a bilingual school, where it should probably be introduced in the third secondary year.

In part III of *Language in Use* most of the units may be readily adapted to cover the two-language complications in a bilingual society. H9, 'Being tactful', can be used to discuss whether Welsh-speakers should use their native language in company containing monoglot English-speakers. Are there special circumstances which could excuse what would otherwise be seen as rudeness? Does the need to preserve and foster a minority language permit the creation of special rules for social behaviour? Such questions can stimulate lively discussion in classes of mixed linguistic background, for the differing points of view are represented and the relevant factors are therefore easy to identify. An examination of the language behaviour of crowds (J3) can start as suggested in the unit by pooling of general ideas about crowds but can then move on to consider the distinguishing features of a Cup Final crowd at Wembley in contrast to the crowd at Cardiff Arms Park for a Rugby international between Wales and England. Are the similarities greater than the differences? Are the bilingual language factors in Cardiff submerged by other features, bearing in mind that the majority will be English-speaking monoglots with perhaps a smattering of Welsh? Is the Welsh-speaking crowd at the National Eisteddfod distinguishable in behaviour because of

79

its language or because of the different nature of the occasion? And so on.

The work of J7, 'Family talk', also acquires greater scope in a bilingual community, for in Wales there is a clear tendency for W1 children to use more Welsh with older people, so that a study of language habits in the home reveals the usual monoglot features but also language choice based on a new kind of generation gap. As always, the teacher is drawing upon the language experience of the pupils, making their knowledge conscious and helping them to see the significance of the various factors, thereby increasing their language awareness. In this case we are concerned with the vital role of language in social relationships, but theme K focuses more sharply on social organizations, including schools and colleges (K1). Language is 'used to give cohesion and continuity to the life of large social institutions', but what happens when we have two languages in the community as a possible source of friction and conflict? Once again a new dimension is added, and one which is most pertinent to the daily lives of the pupils. Similarly, a study of negotiating (K3) is relevant to the bilingual situation in which a minority group is demanding its rights as in Canada or Wales, where the efforts of the Welsh Language Society and Plaid Cymru, for example, provide plenty of language study material. One topic to be covered here is the use of language as a flag. K10 also raises some of the burning issues in a bilingual community, for not only are we concerned with the style and tone of government forms and announcements but whether these should always be bilingual and perhaps with the niceties of argument about which language should come first. It would be possible to continue in this way to demonstrate the value of this approach to language in bilingual secondary schools as in others, but sufficient examples have been given to make the point.

Language in Use is a first, major step in the right direction, but obviously it is not a complete answer. It was designed for mother-tongue students and although it can be adapted for use in other situations the task of suiting it to local circumstances is easy for experienced and skilled teachers but difficult for others. It is flexible, so that the teacher can take as much or as little as he pleases; he can use it as part of a course or as a skeleton to be clothed by other materials and approaches. It is suitable for a wide range of age and ability, but as with all but the most rigid of course-books it does not do the job for the teacher and its success depends on his knowledge and skill. Because it is not a course-book, much is deliberately left to the teacher, whose handling of language in the classroom is crucial. It helps him but it cannot answer all his questions, which may range from doubt about the language appropriate to a particular social context to when to stop accepting the child's sub-standard forms. Books will help him, but they cannot answer questions or discuss problems with him. Above all he needs the kind of linguistic perspective to be gained from Language Study, as explained in *Language Study, the Teacher and the Learner*. The next chapter will examine the knowledge and skill required by the teacher in a bilingual community and the ways in which he can be helped to acquire them.

6 The language education of teachers

The success of any educational policy, bilingual or not, is ultimately dependent on what happens in the classroom. Another way of considering linguistic problems in bilingual communities is to look at the demands made upon the teachers, many of which have arisen incidentally in earlier chapters.

We have, for example, the case of the infants teacher whose new entrants have in some cases 'two second languages'; in the same reception class there may well be other children whose mother-tongue is Welsh, but of a kind very different from the school's Welsh, a particular form of the home/school language conflict which may occur in other circumstances; and there may also be children whose first language is English. Classes of mixed linguistic background will be found throughout the school age range, of course, but the problems in the early years are most severe, for language failure, or comparative failure, at this stage will increasingly handicap the pupil's future progress in all subject areas. The junior school teacher has to make decisions about the language medium and when to introduce reading and writing in E2. The secondary school teacher has to control the transition from E2 to E1 methods and materials. All teachers need an understanding of the role of language in general development, and the delicate relationship which may be constantly changing in the case of any one individual. The list of examples may be extended by adding the basic requirements: fluency in and knowledge of the two languages; an understanding of the nature and function of language; a grasp of first and second language teaching approaches. In short, the bilingual teacher needs the knowledge and training of the monoglot language teacher with much more added because two languages and many permutations are involved.

82

In some bilingual areas the task of finding suitable people for training is impossible, and then the only solution is the provision of schemes which can be used in the classroom with only a limited grasp of principle on the part of the teacher, who is trained to perform his duties in a mechanical way. The important decisions are thus taken away from the classroom and made by inspectors, directors or other 'outside' experts. Even where such measures are necessary, they should always be regarded as temporary, pending a proper supply of qualified teachers, though this attitude is a reflection of the tradition in Britain, where the teacher has considerable freedom of choice in methods and materials and is also consulted in matters of general policy. In Wales, therefore, we must be concerned with the kind of initial and in-service training which will best equip the teacher to handle language in the classroom, language for learning. In some ways the requirements of in-service training are more difficult to meet, for new knowledge and techniques are more easily fed into initial courses than they are disseminated throughout the existing profession.

The need is there for teachers at all levels in the school system, but the difficulties are greatest in the primary sector, where most teachers are not Welsh or English specialists. Discussions with junior school teachers in many and varied areas of Wales in the course of the Attitudes Project showed that there is an awareness of new methods and a willingness to adopt them, coupled with a feeling of doubt and limited understanding which leads to a desire for more explanation and guidance than has traditionally been provided. It is wholly unrealistic to tell these teachers that they should read the basic works or take a course in linguistics (though some will do both) in order to understand modern developments in language teaching. Such advice causes despair, for there are so many competing demands on their time and energy—the list starts with child development, new mathematics, integrated studies, environmental studies, creative work and stretches into the far distance. The only practicable solution is for them to have access to the results of specialist knowledge and expertise in a form which they can use in the classroom, understanding the principles involved as far as they affect teaching, and improving their techniques by discussion with others and by contact whenever possible with those who devise the materials. The teacher cannot in any proper sense be a psychologist, philosopher, sociologist and linguist, though he needs to draw upon the resources of these disciplines, for his main concern is to teach children, an extremely difficult task in itself. Language Study has a particular part to play in that it relates the work of specific areas of intellectual inquiry to the problems of language teaching and learning, and it can be pursued in a variety of ways covered later in this chapter.

If we concentrate on the language needs of teachers we can identify two main areas of immediate relevance to the bilingual, the first affecting all teachers, the second the work of those who teach a language or languages. The first is the vast and complex field known as 'language in the classroom' or 'language across the curriculum', best defined as language for learning. It centres on the part played by language in a child's general school progress and the difficulty encountered by many children in understanding and mastering the language of the school. Our attention was first drawn to this by Bernstein, who developed the theory of restricted and elaborated codes, later modified by himself and Lawton and attacked and investigated by many others. The over-simplified version of the theory which has gained wide currency in the teaching profession suggests that the working-class child speaks one language (variety of English), the middle-class teacher another; therefore the working-class child is doomed to failure in the school system. When put in this crude way, the weaknesses in the theory become obvious, because some working-class children do succeed. The controversy over detail continues, but one value of the theory lies in its indication of certain linguistic and social factors in the educational system which merit study, and a number of general points should be made to define more precisely the factors involved which affect work in all classrooms.

We need to be aware that some children are handicapped in school because their language is different from that of the teachers, but it now seems clear that the difference is not so much one of kind as of usage, and therefore related to the social functions of language. These children have a command of the patterns of the elaborated code needed for success in school because they can produce them when required and encouraged to do so, but they are not well practised in them before they come to school or later in that part of their lives outside school. The majority of the children who suffer a language handicap in this way will be working-class, or of lower socio-economic status, to use a term more readily accepted nowadays, because the crucial factors are environmental and a poor linguistic background is more often found at this level. On the other hand, it must be emphasized that the linguistic background in some working-class homes is rich, while that in some middle-class environments is poor. Social class differences provide some general guidelines, therefore, but social class is a crude measure of language skill and needs to be considered alongside other individual factors in a total classroom situation.

Once the children who experience the 'language gap' are identified the school can do a great deal to help them by providing a rich linguistic environment of the kind needed for success in school, by deliberately calling upon them to use the forms of the elaborated code. The school can thus compensate them to some extent at least for the limitations of their language background. Crash programmes are also helpful, comparable to those given to monoglot English-speaking children who enter a bilingual school in Wales in which the teaching medium is Welsh. The crucial period is before transfer to the secondary school; if we assume that the need is established in the infants school, the compensatory work must be carried out in the junior school. Although remedial work in the secondary school is beneficial, the cumulative effect of general school failure makes the task of recovery increasingly difficult.

We do not yet understand this area of handicap sufficiently, but now we are aware of its importance. More and more attention is being given not only to social class differences as outlined but also to the language of teachers and textbooks, as in the work of Douglas Barnes and of Harold Rosen and the London Association for the Teaching of English. This extensive and deep study goes further than the usual concern over the art of questioning and of stimulating discussion, important as these areas are, and covers not only non-questions or pseudo-questions such as, 'That's right, isn't it?' but also the function of the 'closed' question to which there is only one acceptable answer as opposed to that of the 'open' question, for example. Especially harmful is the habit of never accepting the child's own verbal formulation of the answer, insisting on the precise form of words in the teacher's mind. Language is too often taken for granted by many teachers, including unfortunately some language teachers, who have less excuse. Courses on 'language for learning' should be included in the initial training of all teachers, and should figure prominently in in-service programmes, run on seminar lines to take advantage of the practical experience of those attending.

All this is true of the teaching situation everywhere, but as always it has added significance in a bilingual community. The complications caused by two languages of varying and perhaps changing status have been covered already, and the reader can relate what has been written above to many of the points made earlier. But one particular feature of some bilingual communities merits special mention. In the situation which includes one minority and one world language, there is a tendency for the native speakers of the minority language to include a greater proportion of low socio-economic status than holds for the population as a whole. Moreover, a similar high proportion will live in rural rather than urban areas, and these disadvantages, for such they are on average, are added to the difficulties and special problems faced by the bilingual child in school, calling yet again for greater insight and skill on the part of the teacher. This is the situation in Wales, but it is even more serious in, for example, the Outer Hebrides (Scotland) and amongst the Maoris in New Zealand. Study of the problems is in hand, and the work of the Welsh Language Unit of the Schools Council Project in Compensatory Education, due for publication in 1974, will make one contribution to our understanding of the problems and our search for solutions.

The second major area is the language education of those teachers who will be teaching the L1 and/or L2 as part of their work in the primary school or as specialists in the secondary school. The central task is to gain acceptance for the newer approaches to language learning and teaching which have developed over the last twenty years and which are based on modern linguistics. Some will read such books as *The Linguistic Sciences and Language Teaching* and *The Use of English* (Quirk), and some specialists will tackle the basic works of, say, Fries and Chomsky, but books alone are not the answer, for they demand more time than most teachers can find and they still leave many areas of interpretation in classroom terms. Books like *Exploring Language* and those in the present series are more likely to be read, and have an important part to play, but they need a framework of discussion and experimentation. The principles are the same for all languages, of course, and in the bilingual situation any insight and knowledge gained in the study of one language will have a beneficial effect on the other and improve the total language education of the children. Bilingual teachers may also have a special need, for sometimes they are less sure in their L2 than they would like to be. This applies equally to the W1 teacher

86

dealing with English and the E1 teacher handling Welsh, and it is not usually a lack of basic fluency so much as a restriction in range, a limited experience of and in the second language, reinforced by the tendency of bilinguals to return as teachers to their native areas, something which is understandable but which has disadvantages as well as obvious advantages. It means that such teachers need more help in the various ways suggested than their monoglot colleagues, but the assistance required is the same in kind as for all language teachers.

The solution is straightforward in principle for students in training, for in addition to the general language courses mentioned above they should take courses in the nature and function of language and language teaching methods as appropriate. Lectures and books have a place in these courses, but of greater importance is seminar work to discuss the basic ideas presented and later to report and exchange views on classroom experience. Not all students will be easily convinced, for their own schooling may have confirmed them in traditional views of language and language teaching, so that they are determined to teach grammar as found in the older course-books because 'children must know the structure of the language before they can use it properly'—even though their own knowledge of grammar has faded into their 'O' Level past. The arguments are familiar and need not be covered here. Some few students will remain firm in their refusal to reconsider and will be supported in their views by practice in some schools, but the majority are open to new ideas and will profit from a course based, for instance, on one of the alternative schemes offered by *Language in Use* or developments from it, continuing to build on this foundation when they are no longer students. Language Study and working with language of students should maintain and extend the approach already recommended in Chapters 4 and 5 for secondary school pupils.

The problems and difficulties are different for serving teachers, as suggested earlier, and we must be realistic in our approach. The welcome spread of teachers' centres and the development of in-service training which have both occurred in recent years will no doubt continue to make the task easier by the provision of expert advice and assistance, financial support and release during school hours. As many teachers as possible should be encouraged to attend courses and conferences on language in education, covering the various aspects mentioned, but for some time the proportion of those who can do so will remain small when measured against the total potential audience. Dissemination of new ideas will take place as a result of the efforts of new entrants and experienced teachers who have attended courses and conferences or who have taken diplomas and higher degrees, but we must not be complacent or resigned in our acceptance of this comparatively slow spread of ideas.

The best hope of quicker progress lies in local action, particularly appropriate in a bilingual country where conditions may vary from area to area. Teachers should be given every opportunity and assistance to form study groups, which may be quite small and can meet in Teachers' Centres or other convenient places, to examine and discuss language and the practical problems of language in the classroom, with experts available to help when necessary. Some groups should be restricted to those teaching one age-group, others should deliberately include both junior and secondary teachers, because too often continuity is lost at the age of transfer. The essence of the study-group approach is the chance to explain and explore ideas, to go away to think and try out in practice, to come back and report for further discussion. Such groups will preferably choose their own topics and methods of working, but four basic lines of approach may be suggested as profitable and covering necessary fields.

1. Discussion of concepts of or quotations about language.

This is more direct and usually more immediately helpful than the alternative approaches of an introductory explanation by an outside speaker, followed by discussion, and the consideration of a book or part of a book previously read by all members.

Examples of topics which have proved successful when discussing English in a bilingual community are:—

(a) The notion of *appropriate* language as opposed to *correct* language. The idea that there is no *one* correct English horrifies some teachers, who see it as the abandonment of standards, as the permissive society running riot in the classroom. Others accept the arguments justifying the concept but are disturbed by the subjectivity involved, by their inability to provide 'the' answer when questioned by children. The exploration of the concept in terms of classroom method and language behaviour is a lengthy, inconclusive but rewarding process, in spite of the fact that misunderstandings and half-truths are bound to occur and persist.

(b) Discuss 'Language doesn't exist—it happens', in contrast to 'The bundle of language we've got inside ourselves'.

(c) Discuss the concept of 'slovenliness' in speech, with its implied cure like that of older attitudes to mental illness— 'pull yourself together'.

(d) Discuss the striking sentence on page 130 of *Language and Learning*: '. . . they [children] must *practise* language in the sense in which a doctor "practises" medicine and a lawyer "practises" law, and *not* in the sense in which a juggler "practises" a new trick before he performs it.'

Understanding and discussing the implications of this statement take a long time with a group already versed in language study. Members may then pursue the image, perhaps unfairly, into a consideration of whether the knowledge of medicine used as a basis by the doctor, and of law by the lawyer, equates in any way with the child's knowledge of language. And how does the teacher fit into this picture?

(e) From the same source as (d):
'This way of working does not make difficult things easy; what it does is make them worth the struggle.'

2. Working through schemes of units chosen from *Language in Use* in order to cover the exploration of language in an order of priority decided by the members of the group.

The primary purpose of this kind of work is to increase the teachers' understanding of the nature and function of language, just as literature may be studied by groups for personal enrichment, but it may also be linked if desired with classroom trial of the same material.

3. Exploration of practical problems of language in school, covering not only classroom happenings but also language in the personal and social relationships within the school. The plan is to work back from the actual situation to an understanding and discussion of the theoretical basis for the action taken, or to be taken in future, so the initial question should be of the type represented by, 'How do you react when a pupil says (or writes) . . . ?' and 'What do you do when . . . ?'

Actual situations should be used whenever possible, and the number of these contributed by the group will steadily increase as members' language awareness develops. Examples of starting points used with groups include:

(a) What do you do if you hear a pupil (of specified age)

89

swearing in the playground? Why? Is the answer the same if he swears in class?

(b) The same questions as in (a), but this time he does not swear—he drops his aitches.

(c) What do you say to the pupil who says, 'I ain't done no homework'?

(d) How do you answer the intelligent fourth-former in a secondary school who asks you to explain the grammatical structure of 'He drank himself under the table'?

(e) What do you do about the pupil who consistently does not contribute to class or small-group discussion?

This is a good example of the question which is very difficult to discuss in the abstract, i.e. without a particular pupil in a particular class in front of you. But the contributions from members of a group usually provide a fund of suggestions worth trying out.

One valuable feature of this approach is its appeal to all teachers, including those who are reluctant to examine or discuss theories of language and teaching methods. It is firmly rooted in the classroom and school, and it combines theoretical and practical considerations in a highly desirable way.

4. The development of local schemes of classroom work based on national materials such as *Language in Use*, or *Breakthrough to Literacy*. This may be done by the members of a single language department in a large comprehensive school, but a wider circle of experience is usually beneficial, particularly for junior school teachers.

The reader can doubtless think of many other suggestions and examples, another indication of the value of the study-group system, which is infinitely adaptable to local circumstances. Study-groups may be small or large, though 15 is probably the desirable maximum size, they may be short-term for a specific purpose, or of longer duration, they may be part of an in-service programme or may be formed on the initiative of a single teacher. The aspect of fundamental importance is the interchange of ideas and experience, giving the chance to raise questions and work towards informed answers. In itself this means that the nature and purpose of a group may change, sometimes rapidly, during its existence. The flexibility of study-groups is of special benefit in bilingual communities, many of which are remote and easily isolated by bad weather in winter. This is true of Wales, where in addition some journeys are inconvenient and tedious even in good weather because of the mountainous nature of the country.

In these circumstances the pattern will vary from locality to locality, in accordance with geography and linguistic background. There may be a large group broken into smaller units in an anglicized area in the south, and a small group based on one secondary school and its contributing primary schools in a bilingual area in the north-west, for example. Some groups will deal with the Welsh language and teaching methods, others with English, and yet others with both languages. Some will concentrate on first-language work, others on second-language. Certain groups will be concerned with all the different aspects in turn, others will restrict their attention to one or two of them. Not all groups will flourish, but overall they give the best chance of rapid dissemination of ideas and solutions.

The supporting background to this is the work of the linguist, the literary critic, the philosopher, the psychologist and the sociologist, and the results of educational research and development, providing theories, structures and materials which can be examined, selected and used in the classroom. A proper understanding of language teaching and learning can be gained only by Language Study, as defined and explored in this series. Language Study gives the teacher a greater awareness of the nature and function of language and throws light on the many difficulties of working with language and studying language with pupils and students; in short, it gives him a linguistic perspective which informs all his language work. Nowhere is this needed more than in bilingual education, which faces the teacher with many problems, but which also presents a stimulating challenge.

Further reading

Note: This list is deliberately restricted. Those who wish to read more widely and deeply will find many further suggestions in the works recommended.

See also the list on page 4 of books in this Explorations in Language Study series, especially:

Doughty, P. S. and Thornton, G. M. *Language Study, the Teacher and the Learner*

Halliday, M. A. K. 'Relevant Models of Language' in *Explorations in the Function of Language.*

Bernstein, B. *Class, Codes and Control Vol. 1 Theoretical Studies Towards a Sociology of Language*. London, Routledge & Kegan Paul, 1971.

Britton, J. N. *Language and Learning*. London, Allen Lane The Penguin Press, 1970.

Central Advisory Council for Education (Wales). *Primary Education in Wales* (The Gittins Report). London, HMSO, 1967. Especially Chapter 12 'Language', Chapter 11 'Welsh in the Primary Schools of Wales', Chapter 13 'English as the Second Language'.

Creber, J. W. P. *Lost for Words: Language and Educational Failure.* Harmondsworth, Penguin Education, 1972.

Derrick, June. *Teaching English to Immigrants*. London, Longman, 1966. See also *Scope Stage 1, Scope Stage 2* and *Scope Senior Course*. Longman.

Dodson, C. J., Price, E. and Williams, I. T. *Towards Bilingualism*. Vol. 1 of *Welsh Studies in Education*. Cardiff, University of Wales Press, 1968.

Doughty, P. S. *Language, 'English' and the curriculum*. Edward Arnold (forthcoming).

Doughty, P. S., Pearce, J. J. and Thornton, G. M. *Language in Use.* Schools Council Programme in Linguistics and English Teaching. London, Edward Arnold, 1971.

Exploring Language. Schools Council
   Programme in Linguistics and English Teaching. London, Edward Arnold. 1972.

Halliday, M. A. K., McIntosh, A. and Strevens, P. *The Linguistic Sciences and Language Teaching*. London, Longman, 1964 (especially Part 2).

Hannam, C., Smyth, P. and Stephenson, N. *Young Teachers and Reluctant Learners*. Harmondsworth, Penguin Education, 1971.

Jones, A. A. and Mulford, J. (eds) *Children Using Language*. London, O.U.P., 1972.

Jones, W. R. *Bilingualism in Welsh Education*. Cardiff, University of Wales Press, 1966.

Jones, W. R. *A Report on the 1960 National Survey*. Welsh Joint Education Committee, 1969.

Sharp, D. W. H. et. 'al. *Some aspects of Welsh and English: A Survey in the Schools of Wales*. Schools Council Research Studies Series. London, Macmillan, 1973.

Wilkinson, A. M. *The Foundations of Language: Talking and Reading in Young Children*. London, O.U.P., 1971.